# bonsai

# bonsai

Peter Warren

LONDON, NEW YORK, MUNICH,
MELBOURNE, DELHI

**Senior Editor** · Helen Fewster
**Senior Art Editor** · Sonia Moore
**Project Art Editor** · Vicky Read
**Managing Editor** · Penny Warren
**Jacket Designer** · Ria Holland
**DK Picture Library** · Claire Cordier
**Senior Jacket Creative** · Nicola Powling
**Pre-production Producer** · Andy Hilliard
**Senior Producer** · Ché Creasey
**Art Director** · Jane Bull
**Publisher** · Mary Ling

**Photography** · Will Heap
**Artworks** · Lizzie Harper

First published in Great Britain in 2014 by
Dorling Kindersley Limited
80 Strand, London, WC2R 0RL
Penguin Random House Group

Copyright © 2014 Dorling Kindersley Limited
2 4 6 8 10 9 7 5 3
004–192790–Jul/2014

A CIP catalogue record of this book is available
from the British Library.

ISBN 978-1-4093-4408-7

Colour reproduction by Altaimage
Printed and bound in China

Discover more at
**www.dk.com**

# Contents

# The art
## of
# Bonsai

Beautiful, timeless, and awe-inspiring, the art of bonsai has captivated enthusiasts for centuries. This is the story of how it evolved, and spread around the world.

# The art of bonsai

For many, bonsai conjures up images of the Orient and ideas of an obscure practice that takes a lifetime to master. The reality is very different: bonsai is a truly international art form that is open to everyone – a challenging combination of technique, artistry, and horticultural ability that allows you to create living works of art that will potentially last longer than your own time on earth.

It is generally accepted that bonsai originated in China, and there is evidence of plants cultivated in containers in Babylonian times. However here an important definition needs to be made: any plant grown in a pot cannot be considered a bonsai. Before delving into the history of bonsai, we should first look at what a bonsai is in the modern age.

## What is bonsai?

Bonsai professionals like myself ask themselves this question every day. Throughout my apprenticeship, working late into the night, the same question was asked many times. It is very subjective and personal: many see bonsai as an oriental art form, some see it as an extreme form of gardening. Others think it is a path to spiritual enlightenment, whilst for some it is a simple hobby. It is all of these things and more. To the question of what bonsai is, the simplest, most profound answer I could come up with was: "it is a small tree in a pot". Within that statement

lies something deep and fascinating: an art form fused with horticulture, taking in aspects of design, culture, religion, craftsmanship, and discipline.

The definition of bonsai can be understood from the etymology of the word itself. In Japanese "bonsai" is written as two words or characters: the first, "bon", means tray or container; the second "sai" means planting. So a plant in a pot could be termed a bonsai – but there is a great difference between a young houseplant in a plastic pot and a six hundred-year-old pine tree, growing in a four hundred-year-old antique Chinese container.

The key difference between a pot plant and a bonsai is the artistic influence of man. Bonsai is created, shaped, and maintained to represent an ideal of nature. Horticultural ability alone will not make a

Azalea                    Crab apple                                      Chinese juniper

bonsai, a conscious thought process must go into its creation; artistic ability and sensitivity is required. Aesthetically, the beauty is in the nobility and dignity with which a hundred year-old pine tree holds itself after a lifetime in a pot. It requires a level of interaction that is not necessary to appreciate flashy flowers or luscious foliage of other plants in pots.

With any form of human endeavour, particularly with art and especially with bonsai, there will always be a sense of the artificial. Here lies a paradox: if the ego is too strong, it becomes apparent in the design and display of the bonsai, resulting in something of obvious artifice and detracting from its natural beauty. But something left to nature will, on the small scale, not appear as beautiful as you might like. This balance between man and nature is part of the fascination of bonsai.

From a Western perspective, bonsai falls between many cracks. It is neither purely art, nor horticulture; neither craft nor science. Bonsai requires an open mind and the adaptation of all these aspects in order to create beauty and meaning. Without an

artistic eye, horticultural and technical talent is wasted; without the ability to encourage the tree to grow healthily and in the correct way, the artist cannot create a living masterpiece. For that is exactly what bonsai is – living art, changing not only with the seasons and time, but also with the artistic input from a succession of keepers. A tree that has been alive for several hundred years has outlived many generations, been cared for by many different people and has built up a rich history of its own, with stories to tell in the fissures of the bark, the bends in the branches and the unique character it possesses. It has not only a past but also a future; an art form that transcends the individual and the immediate.

Japanese larch

Blackthorn

Hawthorn

Japanese prints like this one dating from 1780–1820 reveals bonsai was an established form. It depicts two women and their male servant admiring a plant seller's trees.

## Early origins

It is generally accepted that bonsai began in China. Known as *pen t'sai*, there is evidence of training and container cultivation to give trees artistic and metaphysical value in Chinese paintings from the Sung period (960–1279), in which *pen t'sai* is depicted as a hobby of the nouveau riche. Earlier accounts of bonsai from the 6th century also exist, and it is possible bonsai spread to Japan at this time, along with other cultural and religious ideas such as Tendai and Zen Buddhism. By the 14th century there is firm evidence of bonsai in Japanese culture: in one scroll *Kasuga Gongen Genki* painted by Takashina Takakane (1309), potted trees are depicted in the garden of a wealthy patron. A number of other sources from this time including poems, essays, and Noh theatre present similar images of bonsai.

The development of Japanese aesthetic ideas and other art forms also provides an insight into the development of bonsai. The oldest Japanese narrative text, *Utsubo Monogatari* (*Tale of the Hollow Tree,*

*c.*970–999), offers evidence of the idea that natural beauty only becomes truly beautiful when it is affected by the human touch: "A tree that is left growing in its natural state is a crude thing, it is only when kept close to humans who fashion it with loving care that its shape and style acquire the ability to move one."

## Popular evolution

Abstract Buddhist influences were superseded in the Edo period (1603–1867) by a popularization of bonsai, and a shift towards another school of Chinese thought. Newly unified after years of turmoil, Japan became stable and prosperous, and bonsai culture began to spread among ordinary citizens. At the same time an increased fascination with shape and structure was evolving, coupled with a rapid expansion of tree species with the introduction of over 200 hybridized camellias, and 160 azaleas.

The elite class of monks, scholars, and artists took a slightly different path during the Edo period, with a move away from Zen Buddhism towards Confucian and Taoist ideals. The scholarly literati movement was populated by artists who concentrated on brush-based disciplines – calligraphy, painting, and poetry. The Edo literati scholars of Japan followed the tradition of Chinese Wenren scholars, copying the southern style of painting which

Chinese pea tree

Japanese black pine

Scots pine

favoured landscapes featuring idealized images of trees. One of the biggest influences for the literati artists was the *Mustard Seed Garden Manual* (*Jieziyuan Huazhuan*), first published in 1679, which showed how to paint the idealized images. The same images were then recreated in tree form by literati, who were also bonsai enthusiasts.

The Japanese have a unique relationship with natural beauty which influences all arts, garden design, and bonsai. There is a desire for a supernatural beauty, a distillation of the essence of what makes a pine tree so beautiful. Nature can be random and unattractive – and sometimes a deadly force. In the desire to control, perfect, and idealize nature, the relationship goes beyond the visual approach and into the metaphysical with roots in Zen Buddhism and Shinto, both of which were highly influential in Japan. The impact of Buddhism on the Japanese arts, and in particular Zen, is important when looking at bonsai: often a "less is more" approach to design is revealed. The importance of negative space within the bonsai cannot be over-emphasized when looking at Japanese trees – particularly those

created during the Edo literati movement, which inspired an eponymous genre of bonsai with ancient, thin tortuous trunks and a minimal number of branches. It is the pursuit of the ideal, using as little as possible to convey the inherent nature of the subject, the removal of all that is unnecessary to leave only that which is needed.

## A new industry

By the end of the Edo period there is evidence that a profession had emerged, along with a group of collectors from the aristocratic and merchant classes. Exhibitions were held for connoisseurs and the first real instruction book specifically for bonsai was published. The *Somoku Kinyou Shu* (1829) is a gardening book which features a section on classic pine bonsai and explains the concept of "taboo branches". It sets forth some basic principles for designing a "perfect" bonsai, as well as describing the difficulty in achieving such perfection.

This desire for stylization is a common theme across many Japanese arts such as Ikebana or the Tea Ceremony and can be widely misinterpreted as a set of oppressive rules. In fact bonsai is one of the less stylized Japanese art forms due to the lack of formal schools that dictate style and shape. Instead of structured schools, informal groups such as the Jurakukai in Tokyo established gatherings where bonsai professionals and wealthy enthusiasts could meet and enjoy bonsai displays.

Japanese maple                     California juniper          English elm

## Shows and exhibitions

The exhibition of bonsai became a pivotal part of the art form – and remains so today. The first recorded exhibition dates back to the Tenmei period (1781–88), where pine trees shaped in the traditional way were displayed annually in Kyoto by professional pine growers catering for demand from the aristocratic connoisseurs. From 1912 Japanese bonsai became increasingly organized. A national exhibition held outside in Hibiya Park ran from 1914 to 1933. After the success of a few indoor exhibitions, the national show moved inside to the Metropolitan Art Gallery in Ueno, Tokyo. The idea was to promote the seasonal beauty of bonsai through exhibitions held in both spring and autumn. Many of the exhibitors were politicians, high ranking civil servants, or wealthy aristocrats, giving the impression that bonsai was an expensive and elite pastime. The outbreak of the Second World War created many problems for the bonsai community and the national exhibition took a three-year break.

In the 1950s exhibitions and classes sprang up. Alongside the domestic resurgence, increased interest from outside Japan created a need for more organization and in 1962 a national society was proposed to bring together seven smaller regional and national clubs, finally forming in 1965. In the interim the fledgling Nippon Bonsai Association put on a large exhibition in Hibiya Park to coincide with the 1964 Tokyo Olympic Games. The impetus

this created allowed the association to put on an even larger exhibition to promote bonsai to a national and international audience. Expo '70, the world fair held in Osaka in 1970, showcased bonsai to millions of people. This was the start of the modern bonsai boom and subsequent years show great levels of interest.

## West meets East

Although the West had been aware of bonsai since the 1600s, it wasn't until the Meiji period that it became more widely known. The first contact with bonsai was at international fairs at the turn of the 20th century, most notably in Paris in 1878 and London in 1909. After the Meiji revolution (1867–68) the Japanese diaspora created a sizeable community on the west coast of North America, which brought the practice of bonsai to the West, and over time clubs and teachers emerged. But perhaps the biggest influence on modern Japanese and Western bonsai occurred in the post-war period when the interest of occupying forces sustained a bonsai community on the verge of collapse. Over ten years after 1945 hundreds of thousands of Americans and Europeans spent time in Japan, and many continued their interest in bonsai on their

Japanese holly                    Chinese elm                    Rocky Mountain juniper

return home. Several books were published during the 1950s, and in the 1960s and 1970s clubs and societies sprang up all over the world. Exhibitions, conventions, and workshops remained the places to share ideas, knowledge, and techniques, with teachers from Japan travelling to Europe and America in the 1980s disseminating knowledge and ideas.

## Global developments

Bonsai is practised across the globe, but it is thought that the highest level of enthusiasm, talent, and trees outside Asia are found in Spain, Italy, and more recently in the United States. This is in part due to the climate and surroundings as much as their artistic nature. The availability of quality collected material (*yamadori*) and a climate conducive to the rapid development of trees is as intrinsic to the improvement of bonsai as a group of committed enthusiasts and professionals. The difficulty of importing plants, distance, and difference in growing conditions across the United States has led to a fragmented development.

The climate offers a vast range of species, from tropical plants such as *Ficus*, buttonwood, and *Taxodium* grown in Florida to high mountain dwellers such as Rocky Mountain juniper, ponderosa pine, and Engelmann spruce. In Europe it is possible to import Japanese and Chinese trees via a non-destructive quarantine process, but regulations in the United States and other countries require the removal of all soil, resulting in a high fatality rate.

Across Asia the post-war bonsai boom left no country untouched. Taiwan, with close cultural links to Japan, was considered a leading light, but recently China has used its economic success to fuel a rebirth of *pen t'sai* as *penjing*. Large exhibitions have been held across the country and a new exciting aesthetic is emerging. Based on traditional styles and techniques, the image is often very different to that seen in the highly refined, more static feel of Japanese trees. Each Asian country has its own spin: Vietnam and Korea for example are at opposing ends of the Chinese/Japanese spectrum, while India developed separately from its neighbours, looking more to the West and teachers from the UK and US for inspiration. With all the exciting developments around the world, the future of bonsai looks to be just as fascinating – and dynamic – as its past.

European larch          Cotoneaster                    Coastal redwood

# Bonsai
# Basics

All the essentials explained, including advice on choosing pots, the tools you'll need, and a calendar of maintenance tasks to keep your trees at their beautiful best.

# How trees work

The knowledge that trees are living, breathing organisms is fundamental to success with bonsai. If you understand the processes at work and provide for the physical needs of your bonsai as a tree, your artistic desires are likely to flourish more quickly.

## The bare necessities

Every tree needs varying amounts of sunlight, heat, water, fresh air, and nutrients to survive. These essentials are collected, converted, stored, and distributed about the tree by its roots and foliage. It is vital to understand just how much goes on in the foliage and the unseen but essential root system; in the rush to create a beautiful bonsai, it's all too easy to be swept away by enthusiasm and prune too much foliage, remove too many roots – or not enough – or provide the wrong kind of soil and container.

Foliage acts as the skin, the lungs, and the energy creation centre for the tree. Through pores in the leaves, carbon dioxide, oxygen, and moisture are absorbed from and expired into the atmosphere. The amount of foliage on a branch and the amount of sunlight it receives determine the amount of energy generated along the branch; if it is insufficient, the branch will die. Trees that lose too much foliage can have a difficult time bouncing back and take several years to recover. The ability to grow is exponential, and the rate of growth can double every year. The more foliage there is, the more energy is created, which can then be used to generate more foliage – and more growth. In general the more active growing foliage there is, the better.

The roots act as the intestinal system. They absorb nutrients and moisture from the soil, and transport them to the foliage where they are used to create energy. The roots also store excess energy over winter for use in spring. And as well as absorbing nutrients, they excrete waste products including carbon dioxide and other harmful gases.

Many trees enjoy a symbiotic relationship with beneficial fungi (mycorrhizae). On pines this appears as an almost fluffy white growth covering the roots. The fungi receive carbohydrates from the plant in exchange for water and nutrients that they absorb from the soil – effectively they are an extension of the fine root system. Mycorrhizae thrive in a range of environments but they are aerobic organisms and need oxygen to survive.

For bonsai then, the challenge is to create conditions in a shallow pot that retain water and nutrients, and allow gases to be exchanged, replacing waste gas with fresh oxygenated air.

**Most bonsai prefer an outdoor life** in the fresh air where the foliage can collect sunlight and oxygen for photosynthesis.

# Where trees get their energy

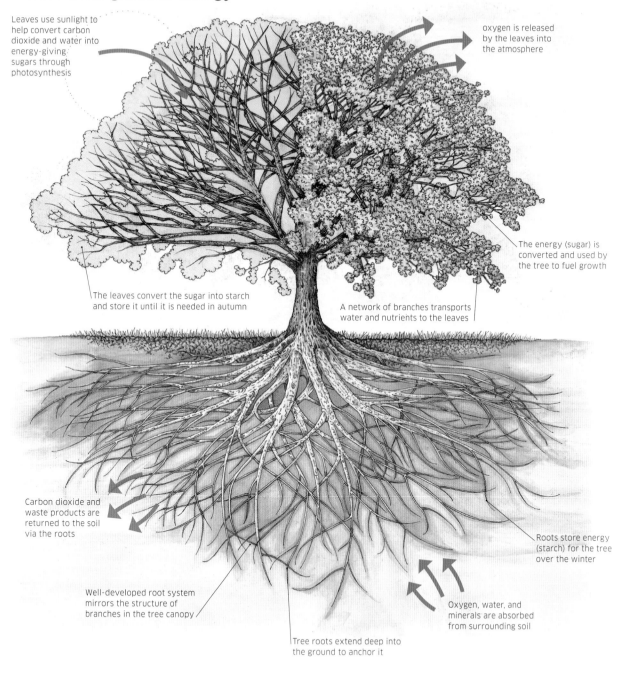

Leaves use sunlight to help convert carbon dioxide and water into energy-giving sugars through photosynthesis

oxygen is released by the leaves into the atmosphere

The energy (sugar) is converted and used by the tree to fuel growth

The leaves convert the sugar into starch and store it until it is needed in autumn

A network of branches transports water and nutrients to the leaves

Carbon dioxide and waste products are returned to the soil via the roots

Roots store energy (starch) for the tree over the winter

Well-developed root system mirrors the structure of branches in the tree canopy

Oxygen, water, and minerals are absorbed from surrounding soil

Tree roots extend deep into the ground to anchor it

# How bonsai works

Creating the correct soil conditions and managing the roots and foliage effectively are the key to success with bonsai. It helps to know the natural habitat of the tree you are working on, as that gives you an idea of the conditions in which the foliage and roots will thrive.

## Creating the right conditions

Some high mountainous trees have evolved to work most effectively in full intense sunlight; others are at their most efficient growing in the filtered sunlight beneath the forest canopy. If these two types of trees were placed in opposing situations they would struggle to survive. To a large extent this is true of all aspects of the tree: the soil type, the amount of water, and fertilizer. However, just because a tree is found growing in very harsh conditions in nature does not mean that those conditions must be replicated in a bonsai environment. A juniper can survive in a very harsh environment but it will also thrive in one that is fertile and more agreeable.

## Soil matters

It is essential to achieve the correct balance between water and oxygen in the soil. Constantly wet soil will cause a build-up of stale air and waste gases that will affect both the level of mycorrhizae and the soil pH, and ultimately your tree will suffer. Too much or too little water also soon affect the tree, so take care. Bonsai pots are equipped with generous drainage holes in the base and these, coupled with a "fast draining" soil mixture, or a layer of large particle soil at the bottom of the pot, not only improve drainage but also ensure that the soil is correctly aerated. It is not so much about pushing water out of the soil as letting oxygen in.

**Wire is used** to secure trees and manipulate branches.

## Roots and branches

In a bonsai pot, the function of the root system is the same as it is for a tree in the open ground. However, the structure of the roots is also very important from both an efficiency and an aesthetic perspective. The root system can be considered to be a mirror image of the branching system above the soil; a well-ramified branch system will be supported by a similarly well-ramified root system, and a tree that has two very strong roots growing round and round in the pot will also have two very strong branches.

It follows that the root system should be set up to support the branching system and growth that you desire in the top of the tree. Removing the tap root at an early age is essential to promote the growth of lateral roots, but these must then be regulated to ensure that they grow evenly across the tree without any single root becoming dominant. The well-balanced *nebari* seen on many mature deciduous specimens has been achieved through regular work on the root system with the objective of creating balanced growth. It is therefore no surprise that the branching is very fine, well ramified, and balanced as well. Pruning the tree's roots is just as important as pruning its branches – however, prune too much and the tree will suffer; prune too little and the tree will not develop in the way in which you hope. One of the best reasons for working with material from a bonsai nursery is the fact that the root systems will have had some work done on them in order for them to grow successfully as a bonsai.

Branches can be manipulated with wire, compacted and moved into a natural-looking postion

**Watering and feeding** are very important, as your tree is not able to call on reserves deep in the ground. Every tree's need will vary. Most like to stay outside where they can receive natural light and fresh air.

**Wiring branches** allows you to manipulate them into more pleasing positions than if they were left to develop naturally. The aim is to achieve an ideal image of the tree using fewer branches.

Lower trunk movement should relate to other parts of the tree; man-made trees can suffer from uniform, unnatural movement – so a trunk may suggest a severe environment but branches and foliage do not

Simplified branch structure is well-balanced for the overall image; reposition shoots to add depth and perspective

**Anchor wires** fix trees securely in pots, removing the need to send out a tap root and encouraging the development of fine nutrient-collecting roots.

**Root pruning** keeps the roots – and therefore the canopy – vigorous and efficient. Fine fibrous roots are important to ensure the tree remains healthy.

A bonsai has a "front" – the best place to view the tree from – generally parallel to the front of the pot

A well-balanced, evenly distributed root base (*nebari*) gives a sense of age and scale and creates the impression of a large tree

# Bonsai styles

A number of recognized bonsai styles have evolved to reflect the growth habits of trees in nature, and these artistic impressions will give you an idea of the variations and their origins. Try not to become too obsessed about fitting a tree into a category – you'll find that many trees fall into more than one.

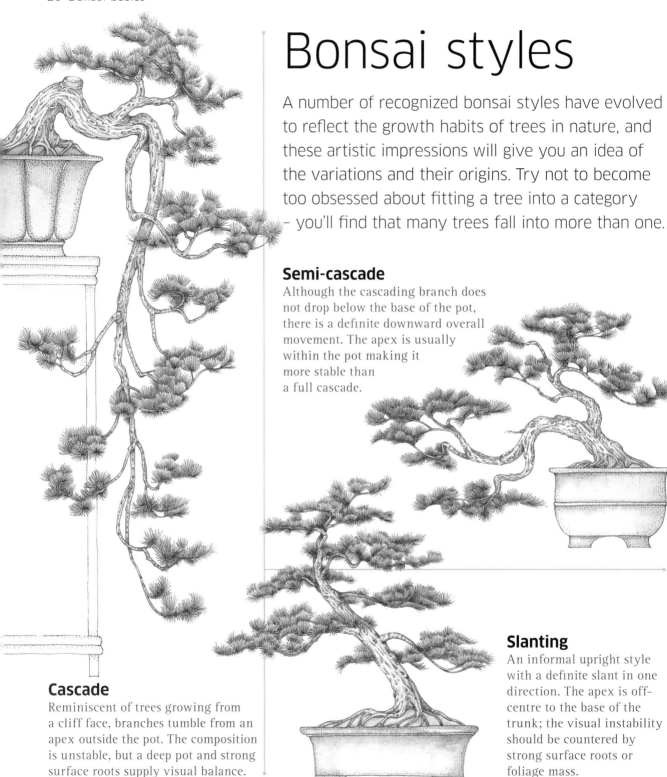

### Semi-cascade
Although the cascading branch does not drop below the base of the pot, there is a definite downward overall movement. The apex is usually within the pot making it more stable than a full cascade.

### Cascade
Reminiscent of trees growing from a cliff face, branches tumble from an apex outside the pot. The composition is unstable, but a deep pot and strong surface roots supply visual balance.

### Slanting
An informal upright style with a definite slant in one direction. The apex is off-centre to the base of the trunk; the visual instability should be countered by strong surface roots or foliage mass.

## Informal upright

Trees that are neither bolt upright nor excessively slanting. Movement in the trunk and the apex position are balanced by branch length and volume to create a relatively stable image with an overall direction.

## Formal upright

The trunk is completely straight with well-balanced branching on either side. Most have direction to left or right depending on branch length; accentuate it with an off-centre planting position.

## Broom

The branches form a rounded silhouette like an upturned broom. They either originate from one spot on the trunk (as above), or along and around a central vertical trunk (*see p.129*).

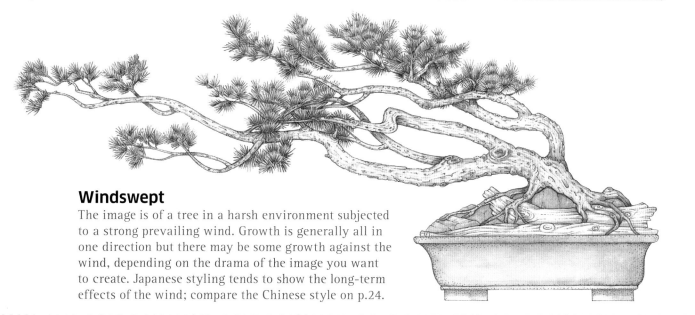

## Windswept

The image is of a tree in a harsh environment subjected to a strong prevailing wind. Growth is generally all in one direction but there may be some growth against the wind, depending on the drama of the image you want to create. Japanese styling tends to show the long-term effects of the wind; compare the Chinese style on p.24.

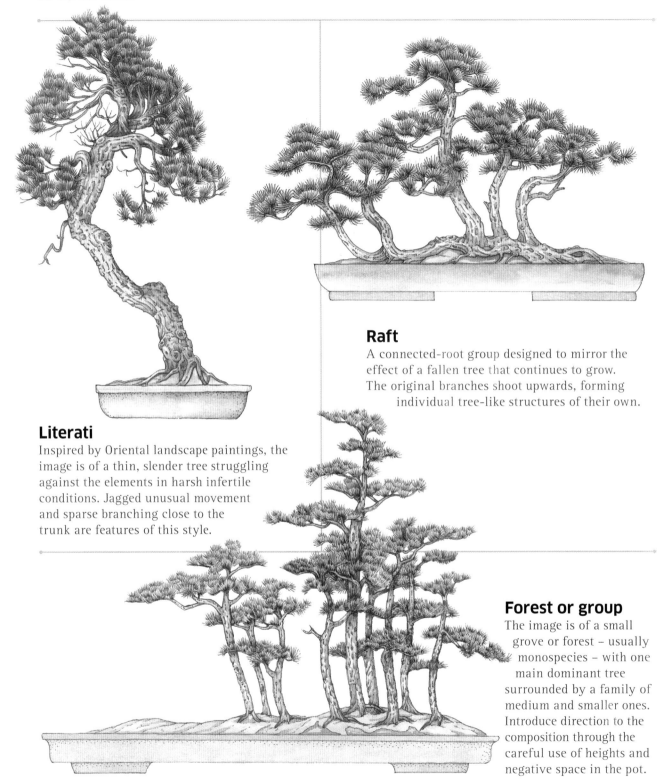

## Literati

Inspired by Oriental landscape paintings, the image is of a thin, slender tree struggling against the elements in harsh infertile conditions. Jagged unusual movement and sparse branching close to the trunk are features of this style.

## Raft

A connected-root group designed to mirror the effect of a fallen tree that continues to grow. The original branches shoot upwards, forming individual tree-like structures of their own.

## Forest or group

The image is of a small grove or forest – usually monospecies – with one main dominant tree surrounded by a family of medium and smaller ones. Introduce direction to the composition through the careful use of heights and negative space in the pot.

### Keshiki

An ultra-modern style combining unusual ceramic containers and young trees to create a contemporary image that works well as an interior design feature. They can often be grown as moss balls (*see pp.164–167*).

### Rock planting

A rock becomes the container, and the trees are planted into rocky pockets, both natural and created. It is often displayed in a *suiban* (a tray without holes). The style of the trees depends on the form of the rock.

### Twin trunk

This features a pair of trees growing from a single base; the triple trunk style is similar. It occurs when two trees have seeded next to each other, or when a very low strong branch grows up and develops into a trunk.

### Root-over-rock

A variation of rock planting. The tree grows on top of a rock but its roots extend into a pot. It is critical that the rock and tree balance in size.

# Styles from around the world

The use of native trees – and mirroring their natural behaviour – is a long-established principle at the very heart of bonsai. It is not at all surprising that new styles have emerged as bonsai has become a global and ever more dynamic art form.

### African Pierneef style
Inspired by the acacias dominating the African landscape – as well as the artist's work – this broom-like style has a more compact "giraffe-pruned" upper branch structure.

### Chinese windswept style
In a stunning contrast with the relatively static Japanese version, the immediacy of this styling creates a far more dramatic sense of a prevailing wind blowing through the tree on a particularly gusty day.

### Flat top bald cypress
Designed to replicate the mature growth habit of the American bald cypress, the tree starts off with a thick buttressed base, and tapers to a few branches in the apex that form a rounded canopy.

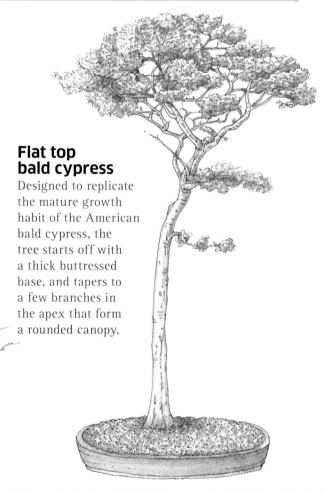

## *Penjing* rock planting

The Chinese form differs
from the Japanese in its more
literal representations of
multi-species landscapes
and the use of figurines
to create a specific image.
It is often displayed
in a shallow marble
*suiban*, with separated
rocky outcrops.

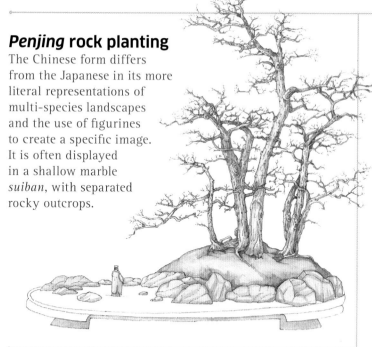

## Chinese literati

Highly stylized and abstract trees with
very little branching. Often seen with
incredibly straight trunks contrasting
with extremely exaggerated and
angular branches.

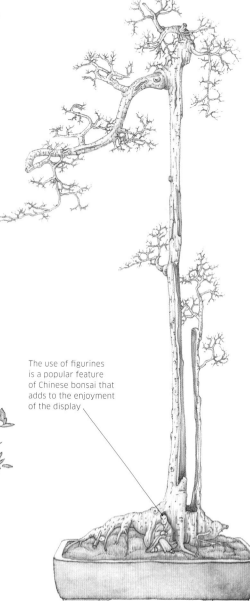

The use of figurines
is a popular feature
of Chinese bonsai that
adds to the enjoyment
of the display

## Banyan fig

In humid climates figs naturally form
creeper-like aerial roots which descend
to the soil and become
solid, significant
roots enhancing
the strongly
buttressed
trunk.

# Choosing pots

One of the Chinese characters in the word "bonsai" actually represents the container – which gives you an idea of its significance. Choosing a pot for your tree is a difficult but enjoyable part of the tree's development.

## Visual balance

There are many considerations for choosing a pot, but it comes down to a trade-off between what is horticulturally correct, and what is aesthetically appropriate for its stage of development. A young tree on its first steps to becoming a bonsai does not need a high quality pot. But once a tree reaches a state of high refinement, it deserves a quality pot of a suitable size to restrict coarse growth whilst keeping the tree healthy.

Once you think of refining the image, an attractive high quality pot is a must. Aim to achieve a visual balance between the tree and pot: this comes from its shape, size, and style, as well as its colour and texture.

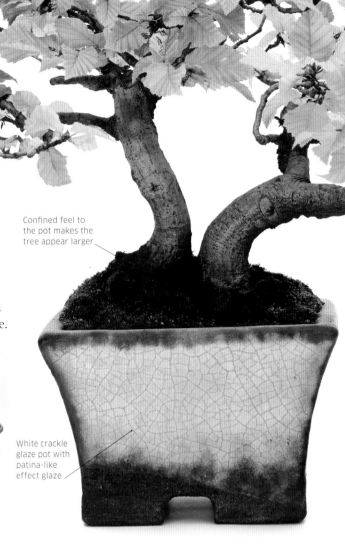

Confined feel to the pot makes the tree appear larger

White crackle glaze pot with patina-like effect glaze

Training pots and wooden boxes are good containers for encouraging rapid development or to rehabilitate sick or weakened trees.

*Autumnal foliage is highlighted by the muted glaze*

*"Finding the right pot to really show off the tree can be a source of pleasure and frustration for bonsai enthusiasts"*

# Practical considerations

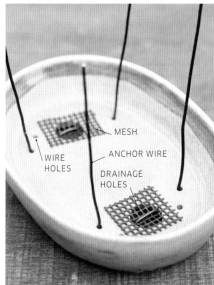

MESH

WIRE HOLES

ANCHOR WIRE

DRAINAGE HOLES

**No matter how attractive the pot**, if it is unsuitable for cultivation, it will be a poor match. Bonsai pots need holes in the base to allow excess moisture to escape and fresh air to enter. Pots made by enthusiasts who know the horticultural needs may have extra holes for anchor wires, but these can be threaded through the drainage holes.

**Understanding the tree's character** is the first step to achieving balance. Look carefully at the tree and ask yourself whether it looks visually strong or weak; masculine or feminine; rough or refined; old or young?

*Cascading second tree is physically and visually balanced by the depth of the pot*

**Pot feet** help to let air in and water out. This can cause instability with dynamic trees, so select deep, heavy pots for cascades, slanting, or windswept trees with the centre of gravity outside the pot.

*Decorative feet add interest as well as allowing air to flow underneath.*

## Colour considerations

One of the most difficult decisions you have to make involves matching a tree with strong colourful features – whether flowers, fruits, or vibrant autumn foliage – with an appropriately coloured pot. To a large extent this is down to personal taste, but it is generally better to avoid choosing an exact match – which can make the tree look drab – and look for complementary colours. Bear in mind that seasonal features are by their nature transitional, so what works for the flowers may not necessarily work for the berries. Unglazed clay pots for conifers are available in a range of shades including red, grey, brown, and purple. They have a subtle but powerful effect on the trees they contain.

*"Deciduous trees are traditionally planted in glazed pots; evergreens and conifers tend to be shown in unglazed containers"*

Autumn foliage will also be set off by the glaze

The naked winter image will feel very cold with a white colour and no foliage or fruits

Red fruits stand out against the cream glaze and green foliage

Age of the trunk is reflected in the patina on the pot

**Selecting colour harmonies** may seem a bit of a challenge: how do you choose a pot that works equally well with spring blossom, summer foliage, autumn fruits, and a stark winter image? Often bonsai artists look to the tree for inspiration, and search for a pot with similar colour values to its foliage or trunk.

Mottled cream glaze adds depth and interest as well as a sense of age

**Subtle textures** can be used to make dramatic statements. Here a *yamadori* pine with incredible flaky bark, crusty sun-bleached dead wood features, and a dramatic cascading form is beautifully matched by a rough pot that almost appears to be hewn from natural rock, creating the impression that it is still in the wild.

Uneven random edge

The rough texture hints at a rugged outdoor life on the rocks

Tall display stand offers additional negative space underneath the cascading branch

# Texture

Often more of a consideration for coniferous trees, the style and characteristics of your tree can be further enhanced by the texture of the pot. Just as colours harmonize or contrast with the tree, texture can be used in a similar manner. In the example shown here the concept of the tree cascading down a rocky mountain slope continues right down the sides of the pot, with a surface finish that mimics the natural variation found on a rock face.

There are no hard and fast rules about planting *yamadori* trees in highly textured pots: in fact they are often seen in very refined, smooth, unglazed containers. The best thing is to be guided by the style of your tree when considering texture – generally formal styles work well in smooth pots that add contrast, and informal literati or dynamic windswept trees suit rougher textures.

## Masculine and feminine combinations

Bonsai are often described in terms of "masculine" or "feminine", and this concept can be extremely useful to consider when selecting a pot. Masculine trees exude a sense of power, solidity, majesty, and strength; feminine trees are slimmer and more delicate, often with finer branching and greater use of negative space. Of course your tree may sit somewhere in between. Ask yourself questions to determine its most dominant characteristics – Is the tree visually heavy? Does it fill a lot of space, or is there lots of negative space within the composition? Does it have dramatic movement or a powerful character? – and then choose a pot that reflects or enhances them.

*"Thick trunks, heavy branches, and dead wood features are typical of masculine trees"*

Branches have yet to fill out but try to consider how well the combination will balance when full of growth

The hexagonal shape, sharp lines, and large lip all add a sense of visual weight

Dramatic heavy dead wood in the trunk; there is a lot of wood in a small space

Internal frame suggests the pot is containing a powerful tree

**Pots with decoration** such as frames, scalloped corners, and belts all add weight to the composition and can help achieve visual balance. You don't want to overpower the tree, but the pot must feel that it contains and supports the tree.

**Often deciduous and always elegant**, feminine trees are at the opposite end of the spectrum, with typical features including fine branches, a round crown, and a smooth trunk. Simple, undecorated pots with clean lines and rounded shapes make perfect partners for trees like these.

It's not unusual for trees to exhibit both masculine and feminine characteristics – for example, a tree may have an elegant shape with beautiful flowing lines coming from a heavy trunk and branches – and in these cases look for a pot that combines masculine and feminine features too.

*"Feminine trees are delicate and light, with plenty of negative space"*

Negative space is a particular feature of feminine trees

The visual weight of a powerful trunk is balanced by the choice of a strong feminine pot

Plain unadorned female pot allows the tree to sing

**Oval and circular pots** are often considered feminine; they look gradually stronger and more masculine with the addition of a pronounced lip, powerful feet, or even a band of nails as though it were a *taiko* drum.

Recessed feet add delicacy to the pot

# Which pot works?

It is easy to overlook as simply being a container to grow your bonsai in, but the combination of pot and tree is at the heart of bonsai design. A fantastic tree can be visually ruined by a poor choice of pot – and equally it can be accentuated by one that is perfectly matched.

An antique Chinese cochin ware pot lends a subtle sense of age and calm to the display, and the depth balances the cascade.

The white glaze and dimensions makes it ideal for a semi-cascade or a tall slanting literati deciduous or fruiting tree

Sharp edges and hexagonal shape are more masculine than rounded ones

The belt around the pot appears to hold the pot tight, as if stopping it from breaking; ideal for a powerful tree

Scalloped corners add a touch of strength

Rounded inner corners soften the strength

Sharp corners and edges create a strong, powerful image

The contrast with the clay texture makes this a very versatile pot

Glazed bag-shaped pots work well with heavier deciduous trees, as their weight appears to make the pot swell

Strong feet add stability

Clean, sharp lines are a sign of formality, so would suit an upright fairly formal pine

Strong masculine rectangle. The lip suggests a spreading image, but the sharp edges add an elegance and masculinity; suits a tall, elegant pine

## Conventional guides

The best choice of pot can often be quite subjective, and this can lead to some unique and surprising combinations. Historically tastes have changed over time, and ideas that were acceptable a hundred years ago would be dismissed in modern times. Over the years however some conventions have endured and although they should not be considered rules, they are guidelines that work well and look very good.

It is most common – but not exclusively so – to see deciduous and flowering trees in coloured, glazed pots, and conifers in unglazed pots. Colours are chosen to complement the character of the tree. The style of the tree has a major influence on the pot's shape, with larger, heavier more powerful trees requiring a more masculine-looking pot compared with the more feminine shapes associated with delicate, thinner trees.

Pot is suitable for cultivation; a more refined, decorative pot would be desirable for display.

Gold repair is a sign of the importance this pot has to a previous owner

The strong lip adds strength to the otherwise feminine round, elegant lines

A rimless oval with subtle colours and no decoration creates a feminine image ideal for a maple or other deciduous tree

Oval shape works well with balanced, rounded silhouettes

A soft rectangle with rounded edges is ideal for a slightly powerful deciduous or flowering tree

The groggy clay removes all formality and makes it ideal for grasses and accent plantings

Groggy semi-glazed clay makes the pot less formal

Oval shape lends itself to feminine trees

Wood firing has given the pot a natural texture and unique variations in colour

Free form shape is completely informal

Ideal for accent plants or for a literati-style high mountain tree

The "nails" in the drum shape provide a sense of strength against the elements

**Carved root stand** adds a sense of drama to a high quality award-winning tree.

# Displaying your trees

Whether you want to admire your trees in the privacy of your own garden or show them on an international stage, a little effort spent creating a more attractive setting for your bonsai goes a long way towards deepening your enjoyment.

## Bonsai in the garden

For optimum enjoyment it pays to set your trees up on attractive benches and create a landscape around them that frames the trees well. Many enthusiasts make rock gardens or Oriental-inspired landscapes; you don't have to go this far, but a dedicated benching area with space, a clear background, and ease of access should be high on your list of priorities. When positioning bonsai in your garden your first concern should always be to ensure the tree will get the right amount of light, wind, and rain. Bear in mind that overcrowding can lead to lower sunlight levels, and makes it difficult to water or spot potential problems. Large trees with their own pedestals make impressive sights and offer easy access to all areas. Smaller trees can be placed together, but think about varying heights, species, and adding accent plants around them to create an attractive and horticulturally correct environment for your trees.

**Japanese-inspired gardens** are often popular backdrops for enthusiasts to display their bonsai.

## Using accent plants

Accent plants are used in exhibition displays to improve visual balance, add a touch of seasonal interest, and also help to complete the narrative of the display. Choose plants that grow in similar environments to the tree and that have naturally small leaves or flowers. There is a class of pot created specifically for accent planting and they are often uniquely shaped with interesting glazes. Growing them on your own benches will not only break up a line of trees, but also adds a very enjoyable seasonal feel to your garden.

**Bold red and yellow colours** make this a perfect companion for an autumn display.

**A multiple species planting** on a John Pitt ceramic "rotten log" sets the scene of an old forest floor.

**Rock plantings** such as this scenic *penjing* display are at their best in plenty of space and a neutral background.

# Basic equipment

A number of specialist tools have been designed or adapted
for bonsai. As your skill level increases and your interest deepens
many of these tools will become invaluable, but for most jobs
a basic tool kit from a specialist bonsai nursery will suffice.

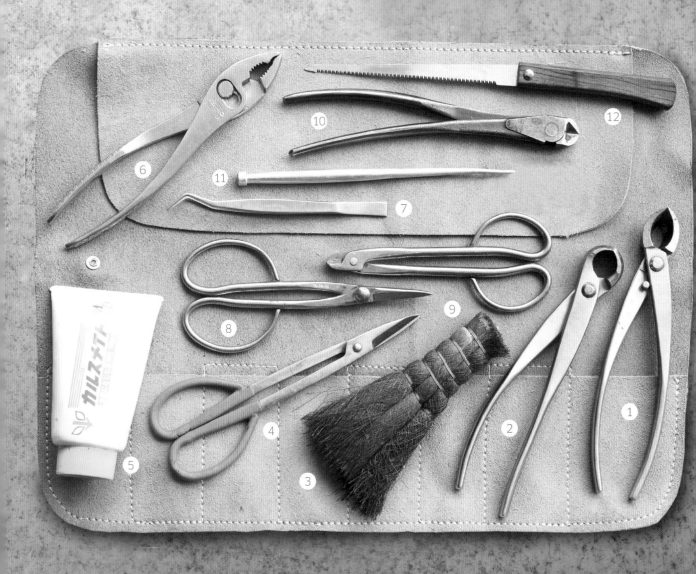

**Branch cutters** Suitable for pruning small branches of around pencil thickness on deciduous trees, and slightly larger conifer branches.

**Concave cutters** Useful for achieving a cut that is more flush to the trunk, and also for eating away at wood that needs to be removed.

**Brush** A small coir brush is useful for tidying the soil surface after work has been done on your trees, and for other light cleaning tasks.

**General pruning scissors** Thin-bladed scissors can be used for a number of pruning jobs, from removing small shoots to cutting fine roots.

**Wound sealant** Apply to cut areas to help form attractive calluses. Pastes may contain antibacterial and antifungal agents, and are easy to use.

**Pliers** Useful for tying wires together when transplanting your trees or using guy wires. They are also used to help create dead wood features.

**Needle-nosed tweezers** Strong tweezers will make it easier to do jobs like weeding, removing debris, cleaning, and needle-plucking conifers.

**Fine-bladed scissors** Thin, sharp blades are an essential for delicate work like pruning fine deciduous branches, or candle-cutting pines.

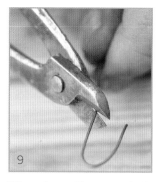

**Wire scissors** These are ideal for cutting smaller gauge wires. Keep them at hand to trim the wire tails when wiring secondary branches.

**Heavy duty wire cutters** An essential tool for cutting and trimming thicker gauges of wire, particularly if you are working with copper.

**Chopstick** Blunt-edged metal sticks and bamboo chopsticks are invaluable for working soil into the roots when transplanting your trees.

**Bonsai saw** The fine edge and thin blade make smooth flush cuts, and give you a greater degree of control than large branch cutters.

# Additional tools

If you want to create dead wood features or do more detailed work, a range of electric- or hand-carving tools and heavy duty cutters is available to help you perform more dramatic transformations.

## Carving tools

It is often quite a challenge to create a natural-looking dead wood feature; to get the best results, use a combination of power and hand tools for carving. Take care when using power tools, and always follow the grain to avoid leaving any tool marks or tell-tale signs of human intervention.

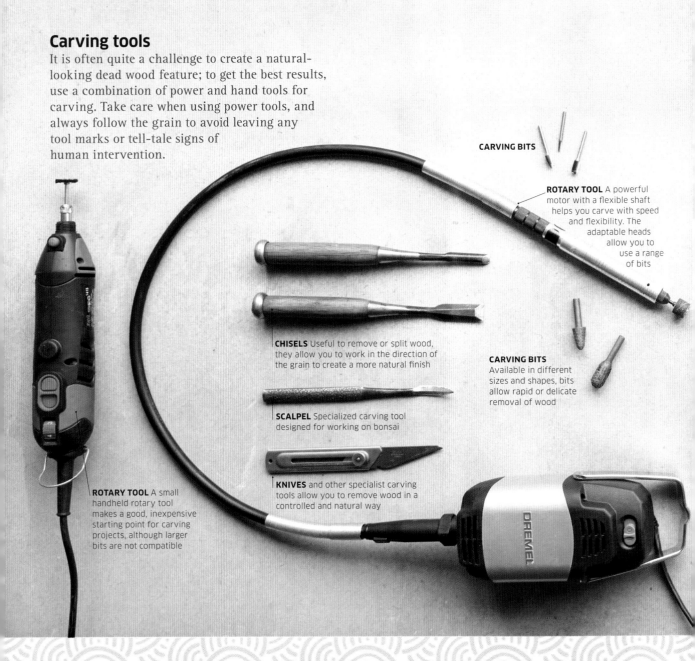

**CARVING BITS**

**ROTARY TOOL** A powerful motor with a flexible shaft helps you carve with speed and flexibility. The adaptable heads allow you to use a range of bits

**CHISELS** Useful to remove or split wood, they allow you to work in the direction of the grain to create a more natural finish

**CARVING BITS** Available in different sizes and shapes, bits allow rapid or delicate removal of wood

**SCALPEL** Specialized carving tool designed for working on bonsai

**KNIVES** and other specialist carving tools allow you to remove wood in a controlled and natural way

**ROTARY TOOL** A small handheld rotary tool makes a good, inexpensive starting point for carving projects, although larger bits are not compatible

## Cutting and maintenance tools

You may also need a few specialist tools for heavy work – especially on older plant material – and for a variety of small maintenance tasks.

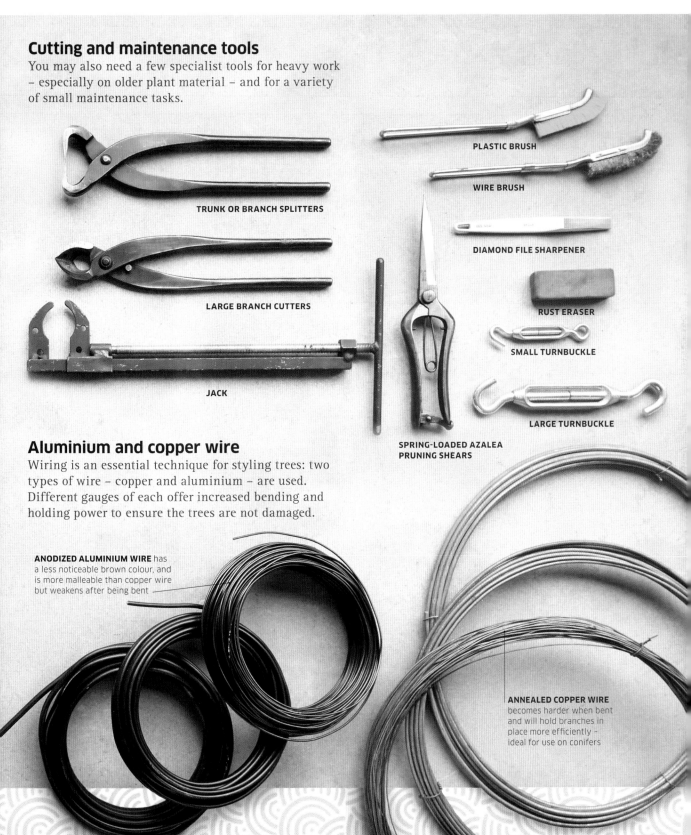

**TRUNK OR BRANCH SPLITTERS**

**LARGE BRANCH CUTTERS**

**JACK**

**PLASTIC BRUSH**

**WIRE BRUSH**

**DIAMOND FILE SHARPENER**

**RUST ERASER**

**SMALL TURNBUCKLE**

**LARGE TURNBUCKLE**

**SPRING-LOADED AZALEA PRUNING SHEARS**

## Aluminium and copper wire

Wiring is an essential technique for styling trees: two types of wire – copper and aluminium – are used. Different gauges of each offer increased bending and holding power to ensure the trees are not damaged.

**ANODIZED ALUMINIUM WIRE** has a less noticeable brown colour, and is more malleable than copper wire but weakens after being bent

**ANNEALED COPPER WIRE** becomes harder when bent and will hold branches in place more efficiently – ideal for use on conifers

# Repotting tools

Removing the old soil from a tree, pruning the roots, and replanting it in fresh soil is a fairly regular job with bonsai. It is a potentially risky operation that requires sharp tools and the correct technique – and some special equipment may also be useful.

**ROOT PRUNING SCISSORS** with larger, heavier blades are perfect for pruning fibrous roots

**CHOPSTICK** Blunt metal or bamboo chopsticks delicately remove soil from the surface and from between the roots

**TWEEZERS** are useful for removing surface soil around roots

**ROOT CLAWS** break down compacted soil. Use carefully, without aggression, to avoid damaging the roots

**COIR BRUSH** used to sweep the soil surface and to remove excess soil

**ROOT SAW** used to cut around the edge of the root ball to separate a pot-bound tree from its pot

**SICKLE SAW** Similar to the root saw, it is used to help remove a tree from its pot

**SPHAGNUM MOSS** helps to retain moisture. Chop finely and sprinkle over the surface

**SIEVE** An essential tool for grading different sizes of soil particles

**MESH** Covers the holes in pots to stop soil falling out

# Soils and other growing media

There is no single perfect bonsai soil. The mixture to use is governed by many factors including your local climate, the tree's age and stage of development, the species, and its care regime. Each component serves a different purpose: experiment to find out which combination works best.

**Sieve soil** to establish its particle size. Coarse grades provide good drainage in the base of the pot.

### Keto
A rich, heavy clay collected from submerged reed beds used for creating rock planting and moss balls. It is not a soil component in itself, but roots will grow into it.

### Akadama
Baked Japanese clay soil with a microporous structure that retains water and nutrients, and assists root development. It can break down after constant freezing.

### Kanuma
An acidic, soft, highly water- and nutrient-retentive soil used almost exclusively with Satsuki azaleas. Easily crushed, so be careful when working soil around the root ball.

### Pumice
Light and microporous, pumice is ideal for improving aeration: it does not break down and the structure enables pockets of air to form.

### Kiryu
A Japanese river sand. Good for conifers, it promotes mycorrhizal growth and retains water. It is often very dusty, so it is advisable to wash it before use.

### Compost
Garden centre compost can be used to make a highly retentive soil, especially useful for young trees to develop lots of roots. However it should not be used long term for fear of creating an anaerobic soil within the pot.

### Volcanic lava
Microporous and light, lava is perfect for improving the aeration of the soil because its structure does not break down and remains solid for many years.

# Basic care

Your bonsai is absolutely reliant on you for regular care, and the two most important aspects are watering and feeding. Both can be difficult to get right: provide too much or too little, and the results can be fatal. Learn to read your trees, consider the climatic conditions, and respond to their needs.

**Careful use of fertilizer** helps to thicken trunks.

## How much water?

Watering is fundamental – but it is also the hardest technique to master. Even experienced enthusiasts can slow down the development of their trees if they adhere to a routine instead of reacting on a daily basis to both the tree and its growing conditions.

- **Every species has different requirements** – and every tree within that species has individual needs depending on its stage of development, and how frequently it has been transplanted.
- **Achieving the correct balance of water and oxygen** in the soil is fundamental for success with every tree.
- **Changing conditions** throughout the year will affect these requirements.
- **Trees use and lose water in various ways**, but about 90 per cent of it is used to regulate the temperature. The tree "sweats" by transpiring water through the foliage: the warmer it is, the more water is required. This is complicated by the effects of drying winds which carry moisture away from the soil surface as well as the foliage. In both scenarios the tree requires more water to replace that which is lost.

You also need to consider the amount of water that can be held in the pot, which depends upon a number of factors:

- **Soil components and particle size.** Small particles hold more moisture than large ones. The soil mix can be adjusted to increase or decrease water retention as necessary.
- **Compaction of soil.** As roots develop and the soil structure breaks down, the surface becomes very hard and less permeable to water. This reduces absorption and can cause the soil to become dry.
- **Size of the pot** and number and size of drainage holes. A pot that is too large will rarely dry out, leading to an imbalance of water and oxygen. A small pot holds very little water and the risk of damage is much greater.

The secret of success is understanding, observation, and experience. Look at your trees on a daily basis, think carefully about the conditions inside the pot and how the climate will affect it, and understand what the tree requires at that time of year.

## All about fertilizer

Fertilizer consists of three main elements and several minor but important nutrients. It has an N:P:K ratio which signifies the amount of Nitrogen, Phosphorus and Potassium it contains.

- **Nitrogen** is used for vegetative or green growth.
- **Phosphorus** is used for roots and flowers.
- **Potassium** is for health, drought resistance, and fruit.

The micronutrients required for healthy growth can be found in organic fertilizers or tonics such as seaweed extract. Avoid inorganic fertilizers: these synthetic mixes are easily overused and may damage the tree. They also have a negative impact on soil microbiology because they kill off beneficial bacteria and mycorrhizal fungi that promote healthy growth. Although vigorous extensions can be achieved there is a difference between vigorous and healthy growth. Healthy trees can withstand drought, disease, and damage; a tree cultivated on inorganic fertilizer may be vigorous but it is rarely healthy.

When applying fertilizer keep two objectives in mind: the requirement of the tree for healthy growth, and your own desire for aesthetically pleasing growth. When a tree has reached maturity and a "finished image", it is unwise to push the tree to grow hard by fertilizing heavily. On the other hand when looking to thicken up the trunk of raw material, providing the tree with more resources will expedite the process.

For deciduous trees at the stage where you are reducing leaf size and node length, and increasing ramification, careful use of fertilizer is essential. A high dose of nitrogen early in spring will result in uncontrollable extensions, large leaves, and coarse branch tips. Instead fertilize lightly once the shoots have been pinched and the leaves have hardened off, and then heavily in autumn with organic high P:K fertilizer.

**Pellets of slow release fertilizer** placed on the soil surface may need plastic covers to protect them from birds.

# Everyday tasks

**Water** the soil – and the tree's roots – rather than the foliage, and adjust the amount according to the weather.

**Weeding regularly** is an opportunity to give your tree a health check, and can prevent problems taking hold.

**Remove dead material** to prevent it rotting on the tree and providing a foothold for pests and disease.

# Seasonal tasks

These checklists are a guide to important jobs that need doing at different times of year. Bear in mind that no two years are ever the same: in mild winters you may be able to get ahead on repotting deciduous trees, but if conditions are harsh, it is better to wait.

## Spring

This is the busiest time of the bonsai year. As the days lengthen fresh growth emerges and new buds swell, ready to burst.

- **Increase watering** as trees emerge from dormancy.
- **Provide appropriate fertilizer** where necessary.
- **Repot and prune deciduous trees** before the buds break and start to grow.
- **Remove winter protection** as the days become milder in mid spring, but be alert for late frosts and protect if necessary.
- **Be aware of potential wind damage** to tender new shoots of deciduous trees, especially maples. Desiccating winds can lose a year of development.
- **Reshape trees that are not repotted.** Wiring can stress the tree, so don't do too much at once.
- **Repot conifers by late spring.** They take a long time to recover, and must be ready for winter.

**Root pruning** is essential to maintain an efficient fibrous root system that results in a healthy tree.

## Summer

Usually the hottest time of year and growth is in full swing, so make sure that you have a good watering and feeding regime established.

- **Defoliate deciduous trees** once their leaves have hardened off. There is time for a second flush of leaves to mature before leaf fall in autumn.
- **Weed regularly**: your bonsai are not the only plants with growth in full swing.
- **Look out for signs of pests or disease** and take action if necessary. Vigilance always pays off.
- **Continue pruning, wiring, watering, and feeding** as required throughout the summer months.
- **Reduce or remove fertilizer** when air temperatures are over 32°C (90°F). Soil temperature is raised by bacterial activity breaking down the fertilizer, so this will prevent it becoming excessively hot, and help your tree to conserve energy.

**Prune long extensions on conifers** to create compact and attractive foliage pads.

# Autumn

Deciduous trees start to prepare for their winter dormancy: many of them will go out in a spectacular blaze of colour.

- **Reduce watering as growth slows** but remember to adjust the regime to the needs of the plants.
- **Check wires on branches** and remove any that look too tight. This is particularly important for pines as they often have a late spurt of growth at this time of year.
- **Protect tender specimens from the first frosts.** Also make sure vulnerable trees such as air-layered specimens are in a sheltered place.
- **Prune deciduous trees to shape** just as the leaves are starting to fall and up to two weeks after. The starches have been transported back into the tree for redistribution to the buds next year; cut back terminal buds before they receive their share.
- **Clear away dead leaves.** Good hygiene is very important; rotting material is a breeding ground for disease and can provide a comfy place for pests to overwinter.

**Wash away algae** so that the trunk does not become discoloured through lack of sunlight.

# Winter

A quieter time of year, but continue checking your trees regularly, and enjoy their winter images. Examine the framework of trees like zelkova and plan ahead if structural work is needed.

- **Watering requirements** are reduced but should not be forgotten. Root activity starts at around 5°C (41°F); do not overwater but respond to conditions.
- **Protect roots from freezing**. Keep your trees in a greenhouse, bury the pot in the ground or in milder climates wrap pots in bubble wrap.
- **Larches can be wired** while their branches are bare, but do not as a rule manipulate other deciduous trees as they are very brittle in winter.
- **Make preparations for repotting in spring;** if the weather is mild enough, you can get ahead.
- **If necessary spray with winter wash** (1 part lime sulphur to 20 parts water) to kill dormant pests.

**Help waterlogged pots to drain better** by placing them at an angle so water runs off the surface.

# Occasional tasks

The secret of success with bonsai is to do a little work often and cultivate your trees on an "as and when" basis – after all, nature does not stick to a rigid schedule. Fit these tasks in when they need doing: some can be left longer than others, but always keep them in mind.

### Housekeeping and cleaning
Good hygiene is essential. Remove yellowing needles, dead branches, and weeds as soon as you see them.

- **Disinfect your benches** each winter. If you keep trees in a greenhouse or polytunnel, disinfect the area both when the trees come out in spring and before they go back to reduce the risk of fungal problems.

- **Sterilize tools** regularly and keep the toolbox clean. Pathogens can be transferred between trees on tools, so this is particularly important when dealing with diseased material and easily infected species.
- **Clean pots** after repotting to remove dirt and hand prints, but avoid removing the patina of age.
- **Clean and treat dead wood** to prevent rot. Look for areas in touch with the soil, or where water collects.

## Unwiring

Wire stays on the tree until it needs to come off; this depends on the species, age, vigour, and amount of bending involved. Some trees thicken so fast wires come off in a month; others so slowly that years can pass. If wire is removed too soon the branch may return to its original position. When wire starts to bite in one place, check the branches that were most heavily bent before unwiring the whole tree.

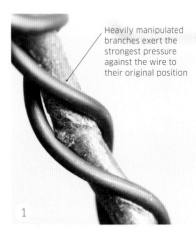

Heavily manipulated branches exert the strongest pressure against the wire to their original position

**Wire is just biting into the bark.** Left any longer this could cause almost irreparable damage. The tree should stay in place once the wire is removed.

Unwire branches in reverse order, starting with the thinnest wires

Avoid cutting off the wires as this can cause damage

**Use pliers to unwind the wire.** Make sure you support the branch just behind the wire to prevent it twisting. Avoid damaging small branches and buds.

**Remove the wire.** Take care around junctions of branches wired in pairs: always leave the anchor point to last, and keep hold of both ends of the wire.

# Bleaching dead wood

Keep dead wood features clean and true to their natural state. Mountain junipers are bleached by intense UV light, but dead wood on lowland trees is dark and rotten. Aim to preserve the character and beware of rotting that degrades the features.

**Clean off the dead wood** with a wire brush to remove soft fibres, dirt, and algae that build up in wet climates. Let newly created dead wood features dry out before applying lime sulphur.

Lime sulphur sterilizes and colours the wood; it turns white as it dries, so try not to overdo it and create unnatural looking features

**Apply dilute lime sulphur** (3 parts water to 1 part lime sulphur) to dead wood with an acrylic brush. Take care: the solution stains everything it touches. Avoid drips falling on to the pot.

Carefully treated dead wood features accentuate and contrast with the live vein

## Winter and summer plant protection

Many bonsai species are strong and resilient, but once in a pot they are in a new and more precarious environment. Life in a pot raises many issues and sensitivity to soil temperatures is one of the biggest. Wild mountain trees are protected by a covering of insulating snow which keeps the soil temperature relatively high, but a pot subjected to freezing air will soon have frozen soil – and expanding water particles cause root damage. In summer, dark heat-absorbing pots can increase soil temperatures to fatal levels which then cause problems for the tree and make its roots susceptible to root-rotting pathogens.

- **Protect trees from extreme air temperatures** – below -5°C (23°F) and above 35°C (95°F). Delicate trees may need protection below 5°C (41°F) and over 30°C (86°F).
- **Use shade cloth** to protect trees from intense heat in summer – but avoid over-use once these conditions pass or you will have leggy foliage and growth.
- **Winter protection** is mainly about soil temperature.

Bury pots in the ground or move to a greenhouse. Do not overheat dormant trees. Light frosts do not affect most trees, but a deep hard frost will.
- **On trees left outside in snowfall**, do not allow more than 5cm (2in) of snow to sit on the branches as the extra weight will damage them.

## Planning

Make a plan for every tree and stick with it: there is no mileage in changing a valid design and setting back development although a lost branch may cause a redesign. Plan for the future throughout the year:

- **Observe deciduous trees over winter** and think about future design. Identify problems and solve them at the correct time of year.
- **Look for pots** so they are ready for repotting. Buy pots you love in anticipation of finding a tree.
- **Keep your tools sharp** and stock up on supplies of soil, wire, and other consumables.

# Troubleshooting

Many bonsai species are accustomed to surviving in harsh environments, and consequently they tend to be less susceptible to pests and diseases. With good hygiene, an understanding of how plants grow, and an awareness of potential threats, you should be able to keep your trees happy and healthy – but sometimes things do go wrong.

**Some symptoms** look alarming, but galls like this may just be unsightly rather than harmful.

## How to diagnose problems

Close, careful observation of your trees as the seasons change is part of the enjoyment of bonsai. If you know your trees when they are healthy, you are more likely to spot when something is wrong.

- **Identify abnormal conditions.** Look for unseasonal colour changes in foliage, growing tips browning off, spots appearing on leaves, or physical signs of insects such as webs – spiders are your friends, but spider mites are not. Dead foliage or branch loss is a sign of trouble. Poor wiring and rough handling damage plant tissue and may cause branches to die. Take care when working or moving trees, and if branches die consider mechanical damage first.
- **Look for progression or a direct cause.** If leaves turn crinkly and brown after a hot day and inadequate watering, it is human error. If foliage discolours after spraying, then perhaps the plant is injured.
- **Over- or under-developed foliage**, fruits, or roots are not normal; look closer if a first flush of leaves is too small.

- **Monitor the soil.** If it is constantly wet, the roots may not be taking up enough moisture and your tree will suffer.
- **Deal with problems in your garden and its trees**. There is no point curing a spider mite problem on your juniper bonsai if it can be reinfested by the garden juniper it sits next to.
- **Eliminate possible environmental factors** such as wind or sun burn; too much or too little fertilizer or certain mineral elements; chemical, animal, or human damage before considering pests and diseases and how to tackle them.
- **Learn what your trees are susceptible to** – and how to prevent it. If a tree is partial to mildew, keep it in a well-ventilated and relatively dry area to reduce the likelihood of infection. Positioning in your garden is essential: consider cross-contamination as well as sun, wind, and humidity and do the best you can in the circumstances. Understanding how and when fungal spores spread will also help.
- **Consider spraying with fungicides or pesticides** as a preventative measure. Start when new growth is beginning and spray once a month with a variety of different products through the year to protect against a wider spectrum of pathogens.

**Juniper scale** can cause dieback. Spray in early summer to eliminate newly hatched scale nymphs.

**Wire scars** This mechanical damage is caused when wire has been left on a branch for too long before removal. The shoots thicken around the wire, which caused the wire to dig into the bark. The only solution is to remove the branch or wait for it to grow out.

**Spent flowers** should be removed: left on a tree they can cause fungal problems to develop. Also remove flowers on trees like azaleas to prevent plants expending energy forming fruits or setting seed.

**Green spruce aphids** cause *Picea* foliage to mottle and fall in winter or spring. Trees can take several years to recover. Preventative spraying in autumn reduces the risk of damage from these pests.

**Gall mites** Abnormal growths appear on the leaves caused by infection or, in this case, insects feeding and laying eggs. The damage is unattractive but rarely causes serious problems for the tree.

**Red spider mites** affect several species and will cause foliage to change colour as mites suck their sap. Spray with pesticide twice – a week apart – to kill hatched eggs before they reach maturity.

**Powdery mildew** A superficial fungal disease that grows on the surface of deciduous tree leaves, especially English oak. It is unattractive rather than fatal, and easily treated with fungicide.

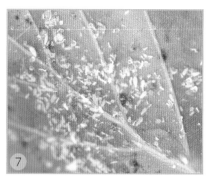

**Woolly aphids** Sap-feeding insects that cause fluffy white patches on branches, especially on pruning cuts. Swellings on young shoots show where aphids have been feeding. Can be difficult to control.

**Winter moth damage** is easy to spot. It is caused by caterpillars feeding on the leaves, which can be quickly destroyed. Pick off the caterpillars and spray with insecticide.

# Top trees
## for
# Bonsai

Advice on choosing trees: what to look
for, and where to buy them. Browse the
galleries of dynamic living sculptures –
and be inspired to create your own.

# Choosing suitable trees

When choosing material always keep in mind the climate and conditions in your garden as well as the amount of time you have to care for your trees, and the level of skill required. Some species are fairly undemanding, but others need constant attention or specific work at particular times of year.

## What to look for in a good tree

If you are buying your first tree, look for material that already has a strong framework and use it to hone your skills. Make sure you choose a healthy specimen: check the roots and foliage for signs of pests or disease, and also ensure that it is firmly anchored in its pot – a sign of a good root system.

- **Start by looking for plants with compact foliage**, especially if you want to make a small tree. Bear in mind that there's a degree of variation within most species: some trident maples will be coarser than others, but all have the same name tag.

- **Look at the relative position, angle, and thickness** of all the major branches. The amount and vigour of the secondary shoots on each branch can indicate how useful it will be. It is unwise to build a design around a weak branch; better to remove it and come up with a new idea based on strong, healthy branches.

Healthy foliage

Weak, spindly foliage indicates lack of vigour, and a possible root problem

Very obvious wire scars

Compact branches with foliage close to the trunk

Leggy growth with very little foliage close to the trunk

Strongly growing trunk

Exaggerated, unnatural-looking movement in the lower trunk

**MIYAJIMA WHITE PINE**

GOOD

BAD

## Assessing trees for bonsai

Always examine a tree from every angle. There are several things that you can correct on a bonsai, but a number of elements that are more difficult to fix. When selecting a tree focus on branch position, the *nebari*, and the lower trunk movement: these factors take a long time – or major surgery – to change. The end of a branch can be manipulated with wire, but the point it comes out of the trunk cannot be altered.

BAD

Strong root that has grown out of the surface

Lower trunk movement is a little too angular

GOOD

Good separation between major branches

No problems with *nebari*

Lower trunk movement appears less contrived

BAD

Large scars on lower trunk

Majority of branches come from one node; this could cause undesirable inverse taper – when the trunk widens at a node where multiple branches have developed

GOOD

All branches have started to ramify

Only one small branch coming from inside curve

## Aspects to consider

Certain factors are very difficult to change without serious amounts of effort or advanced techniques. Use these as a starting point for evaluating the tree.

- *Nebari* The surface roots and root buttress can be problematic for trees that have not had detailed work done. Trees do not naturally develop a balanced surface root system in a pot; often one-sided roots develop. Other problems include crossing roots, roots that circle around the trunk, or aerial roots. Some issues are easier to solve than others, but all can be addressed over time.
- **Trunk movement** The trunk line should follow on from the root base defining the direction and character of the tree. Avoid trunks where movement looks unnatural or man-made, and very straight sections – unless you intend to create a very formal upright tree.
- **Taper and thickness** In most bonsai styles a good sense of taper in the trunk enhances the effect. It can be introduced by encouraging selective thickening, but it does take time to develop. Taper and thickness are often created by making a severe prune back to a new leader and allowing it to grow

**Visit a bonsai nursery** It is in your interest to select trees of a suitable species that have been prepared for bonsai. Specialist bonsai nurseries supply a wide range of material for all budgets – and if you have questions, you'll often discover they are mines of information about their trees.

out; this type of heavy pruning may leave large unattractive scars, but it is sometimes possible to conceal them with dead wood features. Avoid trees with inverse taper, where branches have sections thicker than the trunk that supports them. It tends to occur when several branches are left to grow out from one node and can be very difficult to correct.

**Mature material** can be pricey; be aware that a high cost cannot guarantee success. The projects in this book were all created for less than £150 and all will improve over time.

# Practical considerations

One of the biggest factors to consider is whether a tree will grow naturally in your garden. Native trees are most likely to suit local conditions, but many imported Japanese species grow well in temperate climates too. Consider not only temperature but also rainfall, sunlight levels, water, soil pH, and air quality. If you provide ideal conditions for tropical trees in sub-arctic countries, then some level of success will follow. After a few years of bonsai cultivation you will soon learn which trees do well in your garden and which do not. Try to work out why, and if those factors are beyond your control, focus on species that thrive.

Bonsai is a subjective art form: there is no such as thing as right or wrong. Conventional ideas exist but there is also great scope for variation and personal preference. When looking at bonsai some will interest you more than others. Stop, look hard, and question why and what it is about a certain tree that draws you to it. This will help you to develop your personal taste and identify styles and species that fit with it, even if they are unconventional.

**Trees growing in harsh conditions** such as rugged mountainsides can be a great source of inspiration when designing your bonsai.

Species with small foliage are more pleasing as bonsai

**Buy collected material** from a specialist nursery to ensure it was collected legally and given a good start in a pot.

**This collected olive** has been styled as a literati bonsai. Despite the highly stylized form, the tree retains a sense of how olive trees grow naturally on European hillsides.

# Easy to grow

There is no such thing as a maintenance-free bonsai, but the trees introduced here are less fussy than most, and make excellent choices for beginners. They may be easier to style and look after, but that does not detract from their beauty, nor prevent them developing into incredible specimen trees.

**Resilient, responsive, and forgiving,** the trees featured on these pages will give new bonsai enthusiasts the best, quickest, and easiest results. Often the species used for bonsai can be quite particular about their environment, or require specialized techniques to ensure success, but these easy-going trees have an altogether more relaxed attitude to life – ideal for beginners keen to hone their skills and practise basic techniques, from directional pruning ("clip and grow"),

to wiring and transplanting. Do bear in mind that they are not indestructible, and certainly won't thank you for neglect or rough treatment – even the toughest tree has a breaking point – but for trees that offer plenty of year-round enjoyment and a chance to get to grips with the basics of bonsai, look no further.

Compact, tight foliage ideal for small-to-medium trees

Bright red fruits in autumn and winter

Cascading branch gives the tree dramatic movement

# Cotoneaster
## *Cotoneaster horizontalis*

**Grown for their spreading habit and colourful fruits**, cotoneasters are popular garden shrubs widely used for cover in harsh urban environments. These vigorous plants will send out shoots on old wood, and flower and fruit with ease. They also tolerate drought, but thrive given water and fertilizer. Wire the main branches and prune to shape. For more shoots and increased branching remove the internal leaves.

Dead wood features are unusual, but not unnatural: this old root was exposed when the planting angle changed

Fine root system ideally suited to life in a container

Outwardly curving pot with a small base complements the semi-cascade; strong lines give a sense of masculinity

## Key features

- **Flowers pollinate easily** without additional help; provide food and water, and fruits will be plentiful.

- **Prune selectively** throughout the year, to create the basic structure. The branches will fill out using the clip-and-grow technique.

**35cm / 14in tall**

Courtesy of John Brocklehurst

### Looking closer
Top: Branches bend easily when young, but become more brittle with age.
Centre: The fruits remain on the tree over winter, but do protect them from birds.
Below: Soft dead wood features will need regular cleaning and protection.

# Trident maple
## *Acer buergerianum*

**A must for every bonsai enthusiast,** even beginners will be able to style this tree into almost any size and shape. You can enjoy it year-round, too: in winter, without its leaves, it reveals its fine ramification; in spring, it has eye-catching breaking buds; and in autumn, its colour display is unbeatable.

### Key features

- **Defoliate this maple** several times a year but be careful not to overdo it. If you do, you may weaken the tree or make it grow too coarsely.

- **The Achilles heel** of this tree is its fleshy roots. If you subject the pot to a long, hard freeze, they can be fatally damaged.

### Looking closer
Above: This maple's common name – Trident Maple – comes from its small, three-lobed leaves. When buying, look for naturally small leaves. Below: As it grows, the trunk clings to its rock in a convincingly natural, organic manner.

Removing some external leaves allows the sun to reach the internal leaves and helps them thrive

Autumn colour is a highlight

A superb example of the style of planting a maple against a rock

Regular defoliation keeps the leaves small and increases ramification

The shape of the pot accentuates the tree's movement and supports the weight of the rock and the trunk

**35cm / 14in tall**

**Courtesy of John Pitt**

# Chinese elm
## *Ulmus parvifolia*

**Readily available from garden centres** and other outlets, this is the bonsai that many make their first buy. It is sometimes considered rather ordinary, but if you are patient and plan carefully, you can grow it into a stunning specimen, with very fine, well-ramified branches and attractively aged bark.

### Key features

- **Tolerant** of a wide range of climates, this elm can even withstand drought.

- **If grown indoors,** give plenty of sun but keep away from direct heat, especially radiators.

- **Regular, directional pruning** – "clip and grow" – encourages growth in the desired direction.

Grow this very tough deciduous bonsai indoors or out

Use defoliation to make the naturally small leaves even smaller

Cork bark adds character and will develop on some cultivars

The oval pot complements the elm's well-rounded branching structure

### Looking closer
Above: You can prune the roots back fairly hard initially to create a fine root system. After that, aim to prune the root growth to create a well-rounded *nebari*. Below: Small leaves mean small, delicate branches. Give them warm conditions and they will grow almost all year round.

**22cm / 9in tall**
Courtesy of John Brocklehurst

# Potentilla
## *Potentilla fruticosa*

**The highlight of this beautiful shrub** is its mass of dainty yellow and orange flowers. Thanks to its resilience, the potentilla is also a superb choice for bonsai. You can prune it back hard and it will send out buds from the old wood. Fine branches readily develop from pruning alone, and if you want to make a feature of attractive dead wood and interesting trunk lines, removing lots of branches is the way to go. A great choice for year-round interest.

**40cm / 16in tall**
Courtesy of Peter Warren

Rounded silhouette in the apex created by pruning longer shoots

Shoot tips may die off in frost, but new buds emerge all over the branches and trunk

Dieback has created an interesting hollow and a *shari* effect on the trunk

Develop and thicken the cascading branch by leaving it unpruned

This Ron Lang pot is deliberately placed corner-on to the front to provide an angular counterpoint to the sinuous movement

### Looking closer
Top: New buds form readily on old wood in the wake of frost damage or after pruning.
Centre: Flowers vary depending on the cultivar. Remove dead flowers before they turn to seed and sap the tree's energy.
Below: Collected specimens may feature sinuous live veins and hollowed-out trunks; visit reputable bonsai nurseries to find interesting material.

### Key features
- **Flowers develop at the end of new shoots.** If you want to focus on the flowers, do not prune the new growth, and fertilize after flowering. If you want vegetative growth, fertilize early and prune to shape.

- **Branches soon become brittle and cannot be bent,** so set the basic skeleton, then use scissors and directed growth for further shaping.

# Chinese juniper
## *Juniperus chinensis*

**Junipers are one of the most frequently used trees** for bonsai and the Chinese juniper is their poster child. Part of the attraction is its distinctly oriental look, but its popularity must also lie in the fact that its trunk and branches are both extremely flexible and respond well to shaping. Rounded foliage pads complement the tree's sinuous lines and deadwood features.

20cm / 8in tall
Courtesy of
John Armitage

Image is of a dragon twisting through the clouds

## Key features

- **This lovely tree responds well to wiring** and you can carry out wiring at any time of year.

- **Never remove too much foliage in one go.** Junipers are particularly sensitive to losing their leaves and will respond by producing a mass of undesirable juvenile growth.

Carved dead wood is a great foil for the shaggy red-brown bark

Contrast between live vein and dead wood shows the severity of the natural world

Foliage pads on this side balance the dead wood features on the other

## Looking closer
Top: The *shari* trunk has been carved by hand to recreate natural dead wood.
Centre: Dense compact foliage is characteristic of this popular 'Itoigawa' variant.
Below: Dead wood is carefully created by reading the flow of the live vein from root to branch and removing sections that are not necessary.

# Evergreen stars

Evergreen trees retain their foliage all year round – but despite these well and truly green credentials, they are far from dull. There are plenty to choose from, including many that will flower and fruit as well, but the conifers showcased here are full of character, offering a subtle change of tone across the seasons.

**The evergreen foliage** that distinguishes this group is far more than just a decorative feature: it is a powerhouse that runs all year round to generate the energy which the plant needs to grow. This explains why most evergreens, particularly junipers, will react very badly if too much foliage is removed at one time – essentially you are expecting them to operate in a power cut. Many of the evergreen species used in bonsai are conifers. They often require plenty of wiring in order to maintain their shape, but do not let that put you off. Pine trees for example are initially quite imposing but if you understand a few basic ideas, they can be transformed in a very short period of time. The majority of conifers, particularly pines, benefit from less frequent transplanting. Allow them to settle in the pot and develop a strong root system.

Dense, compact and slightly shaggy foliage

Long cascading branch defines the movement, with foliage pads that are deliberately less refined

# Ezo spruce
## *Picea glehnii*

**Rough-and-ready spruce trees** are from colder climates where their branches sag under the weight of snow. Their short needles are ideal for bonsai cultivation, and the Ezo spruce is one of the most compact. Foliage pads are slightly rugged, in keeping with the wild nature of the species.

## Key features

- **Spruce enjoy the snow** and generally endure the cold, but dislike freezing winds. Position them in partial shade in summer, provide shelter for winter and do not allow a deep hard freeze to affect the pot.

- **Wire the main branches** to set the structure. Allow new growth to extend and then pinch off the tips to encourage more shoots to develop further back inside the tree.

The rock balances this dynamic tree, allowing for a smaller pot size

Moss and compact accent plants growing over the root base add character

Warped pot reflects the rough-and-ready character of the tree

Balancing branch close to the trunk helps stop the tree from appearing to fall over

## Looking closer

Top: Young extensions give the foliage a subtle two-tone colour. Centre and below: Accent plants growing on the rock and roots are naturally compact alpine species that would be found in that environment. They can be used to add character, or even to conceal faults.

**45cm / 18in tall**

Courtesy of John Pitt

# Natal fig
## *Ficus natalensis*

**The Natal fig has its origins in South Africa**, so it thrives best in a sub-tropical climate. In fact, given enough warmth and sunlight, it is very vigorous. With the right conditions, it will grow a magnificent set of buttressed trunks and will throw out a mass of striking aerial roots, banyan style. But if you live in a more temperate climate, do not despair; you will still be able to grow a happy specimen indoors or in a greenhouse.

### Key features

- **The leathery leaves** will withstand drought conditions very well but the tree thrives better if you water it regularly.

- **The slightly-larger-than-average leaves** are best suited to a slightly-larger-than-average specimen tree.

- **Aerial roots and a multiple trunk** can be developed with humid growing conditions and pruning.

### Looking closer

Top: The pointed, leathery, oval leaves have reddish, very attractive undersides.
Centre and below: Encourage a multiple buttressed trunk effect to create a sense of age and the impression of a massive old tree. Aerial roots should develop naturally but any that become too thick should be removed or they will spoil the overall look.

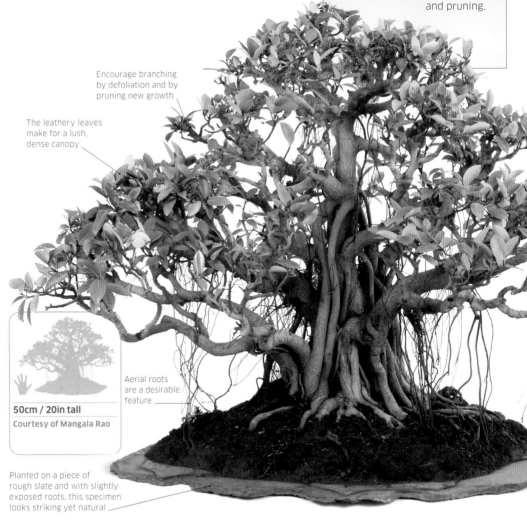

Encourage branching by defoliation and by pruning new growth

The leathery leaves make for a lush, dense canopy

50cm / 20in tall
Courtesy of Mangala Rao

Aerial roots are a desirable feature

Planted on a piece of rough slate and with slightly exposed roots, this specimen looks striking yet natural

# Scots pine
## *Pinus sylvestris*

**If you are looking for a tree that lends itself to the *literati* style,** then this species of pine is one of the star candidates. Nature provides it with a tall, slender trunk with only upper branches, so you are halfway there already. In addition, the Scots Pine is a vigorous grower and responds well to bonsai styling techniques. You will need patience to achieve *mochikomi*, but the rewards are great. It is no wonder that this tree is a star.

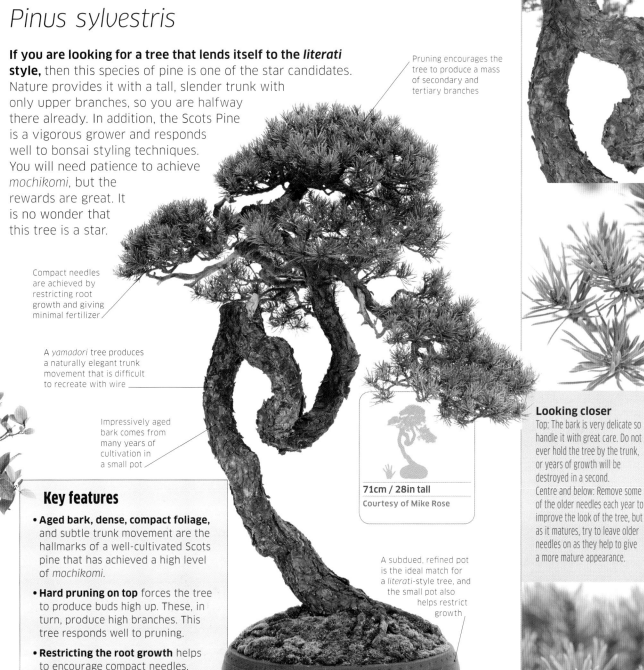

Pruning encourages the tree to produce a mass of secondary and tertiary branches

Compact needles are achieved by restricting root growth and giving minimal fertilizer

A *yamadori* tree produces a naturally elegant trunk movement that is difficult to recreate with wire

Impressively aged bark comes from many years of cultivation in a small pot

A subdued, refined pot is the ideal match for a *literati*-style tree, and the small pot also helps restrict growth

**71cm / 28in tall**
**Courtesy of Mike Rose**

## Key features

- **Aged bark, dense, compact foliage,** and subtle trunk movement are the hallmarks of a well-cultivated Scots pine that has achieved a high level of *mochikomi*.

- **Hard pruning on top** forces the tree to produce buds high up. These, in turn, produce high branches. This tree responds well to pruning.

- **Restricting the root growth** helps to encourage compact needles, which adds to the sense of age.

### Looking closer

Top: The bark is very delicate so handle it with great care. Do not ever hold the tree by the trunk, or years of growth will be destroyed in a second.
Centre and below: Remove some of the older needles each year to improve the look of the tree, but as it matures, try to leave older needles on as they help to give a more mature appearance.

# Japanese black pine
## *Pinus thunbergii*

**Masculine, powerful, compact, and characterful,** this pine is the king of the Japanese bonsai world. It lends itself to a wide range of styles, from formal upright to cascade, and to all sizes. Its strong, sharp needles and vigorous growth seem at odds with the sense of age of its flaky bark, but these opposites actually add to the tree's enormous dramatic impact.

### Key features

- **New shoots can be pruned off** in summer to force a second flush of growth. This will double the number of branches and halve the length of the needles.

- **Make sure the plant's energies are evenly spread** or internal and lower branches will soon die. To achieve this balance, remove needles from strongly growing areas to restrict energy production there and to allow sunlight – and energy – into the weakly growing shaded areas.

**70cm / 28in tall**
Courtesy of
Mike Rose

Uncut candles lead to normal-sized growth and dense, lush foliage

### Looking closer
Top: You can reduce the length of the needles so they suit the size of tree you want to grow.
Centre: Removal of needles has created vigour and brought light to shaded areas.
Below: Grasping roots give a sense of stability that balances the tree's cascading style.

A sense of dramatic tension exists between areas of dense foliage and the aged trunk

Choose a pot that accentuates the masculinity of the tree and the dynamic nature of the style

Sharp crank-style bends add even more character to this powerful, compact tree

# European yew
## *Taxus baccata*

**The dramatic contrast between live and dead wood** is what makes the European yew so eye-catching. You can even enhance the effect by whitening the dead wood. It is a superb tree for bonsai cultivation, especially if you start with a collected specimen like this one. Careful pruning and pinching out of the new growth encourages the back budding you need to create the tree's fabulously dense pads of foliage.

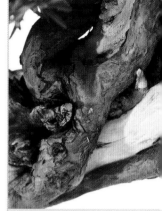

**42cm / 17in tall**
Courtesy of John Pitt

### Looking closer
Top and centre: A swollen live vein growing around dead wood, and the live trunk alongside the dead one, give a sense of the tree's powers of endurance. Below: The leaves are small and the foliage is compact but you should control excessively dense areas with careful pruning.

A foliage pad on this side helps to stop the tree from appearing to fall over in its pot

Whitened dead wood adds texture, and gives a sense of nature at work

The live vein splits and leads the eye upwards towards the canopy

Directional clip and grow techniques keep foliage at the optimum density

A thin live vein runs up the side of the dead trunk

### Key features

• **Taxus grow throughout Europe** and can withstand a wide range of environments, but they do like a little shade in midsummer.

• **The fleshy roots are vulnerable,** so be sure to protect them from freezing in winter.

• **Start by wiring** to achieve the basic shape, then pinch out new growth to promote adventitious buds. Afterwards, use directional pruning to direct new growth.

# Seasonal beauties

One of the great joys of bonsai is the ability to follow the progress of the seasons through your sculpture – from the first optimistic buds bursting in spring, to the last hurrah of vibrant autumn foliage. The trees in this section almost reinvent themselves, revealing dramatically different characteristics throughout the year.

**The most dramatic seasonal change** occurs in autumn when deciduous trees turn shades of yellow, orange, and red as their leaves start to shut down for the year before the tree goes into dormancy. Maples, zelkova, and sumac are some particular highlights for autumn colour, but they also look very vibrant and youthful during spring when their buds start to swell and the new shoots open. Some trees may be outstandingly beautiful for just two weeks but still have aesthetic value as bonsai. Other trees offer flowers and fruit over all four seasons, providing a real sense of the time of year and the cyclical nature of life.

Colourful bracts are a highlight throughout the year

Cascading branch is just at the right length compared to the thickness of the trunk

# Bougainvillea

## *Bougainvillea* 'Blondie'

**These flowering vines** prefer tropical conditions but will grow in more temperate climates if winter protection is provided, and will positively thrive in warmth. The showy "flowers" are actually bracts – modified leaves – designed to attract insects to the actual flowers, which are very small. They are very versatile trees and ideal bonsai specimens for those in warmer areas.

### Key features

- **Withstands heavy pruning**. If growing bougainvillea in a hot climate it is possible to prune back to a very raw state.

- **Flexible young shoots** soon become brittle branches, so it is wise to style them when young. Use advanced bending techniques to style older trees.

Textured trunk improves with age and exposure to sunlight

Deep pot helps balance the cascading nature of tree; a slightly smaller pot could be used to introduce more drama

Lower trunk movement adds visual weight to the base, balancing the cascading movement

**90cm / 36in tall**
**Courtesy of Mangala Rao**

### Looking closer

Top: Tiny tubular flowers are surrounded by petal-like bracts. Centre: Evergreen foliage may sometimes conceal thorny stems. Below: The gnarled silver trunk creates drama and interest at the top of the cascade.

# Japanese larch
## *Larix kaempferi*

**Tiny cones, a straight, slender trunk,** and alternating branches. These are the jewels the larch has to offer, whether grown naturally or cultivated as a bonsai. This deciduous conifer offers a feast of year-round enjoyment. Golden, swelling spring buds turn into vibrant, fresh new growth followed by bright yellow autumn foliage. In winter, the effect of its stark, naked silhouette is softened by the rounded cones.

## Key features

• **Delicate foliage can burn** in intense sunlight so it is important to protect the foliage from the sun after you have pruned the new growth.

• **Allow some length to develop** along the branches between the nodes, otherwise the alternating shoots will be too close together and the result will be growth that is over-dense and crowded.

### Looking closer
Cones start out green, then turn brown, open up, and remain on the tree for several years. Thin them out and do not allow too many to form in one area as this will look unbalanced. Thinning the cones also helps conserve the tree's energy since they can be a great drain.

Bright green foliage follows gold-coloured spring buds

Cones form on the very tips of the branches and add interest

Multiple tall, elegantly slim trunks create a beautiful forest group

Aged bark is roughly textured and attractively multi-coloured

One or two strong roots often develop but must not be allowed to dominate; take care as the tree does not tolerate heavy root-pruning

**88cm / 35in tall**
**Courtesy of Peter Chan**

# Satsuki azalea
## *Rhododendron indicum*

**A myriad of beautiful summer flowers** immediately catches the eye, making this wonderful evergreen instantly attractive. What is more, there are thousands of cultivars, so you have a massive variety of differently shaped and coloured flowers, as well as different leaf sizes, to choose from. And when the flowers have faded, you can still enjoy the tree's lovely shape, foliage, and attractively aged bark right through autumn and winter.

Do not prune the apex back too hard to ensure its strength is maintained

Flower buds on the verge of bursting promise several weeks of beauty

Remove new shoots in spring if they are going to get in the way of the flowers

Avoid a weak apex by not allowing the fine roots to become too compacted

**54cm / 22in tall**
**Courtesy of Ian Cuppleditch**

### Looking closer
Top and below: Over time, the trunk will gently age, giving the tree a subtle, calm appearance when not in flower.
Centre: This is one of many available flower types. The flowers need protection from water, including rain. Remove flowers when they start to fade.

## Key features
- **Even the old wood buds prolifically,** which makes these trees easy to style. And because they are styled against their natural growth habit, you can choose almost any style you like.
- **These slightly temperamental trees** prefer moist conditions, acidic soil, and acidic water.

# Sageretia
## *Sageretia thea*

**With its clusters of white flowers** followed by small blue fruits, this lovely evergreen tree is a frequent choice for indoor bonsai in places with a more temperate climate. It is a vigorously growing tree, so do not be afraid to prune it to shape all through the year using directional pruning. It will reward you by producing a large number of fine side branches and will even send out buds from the old wood.

**63cm / 25in tall**
Courtesy of Hoka-en

**Looking closer**
Top and bottom: The multi-coloured branching trunk is a key feature. The trunk of this specimen has attractive hollows and calluses.
Centre: The dainty oval leaves are shiny and attractively veined. They are carried on the tree's mass of fine branches.

The tiny leaves are almost bronze when they first appear

Pruning to shape will give a mature, flattish canopy

Branches tend to be rather thin with many fine secondary and tertiary branches

Clean and preserve the soft dead wood to prevent it rotting

The mature trunk is multi-coloured

## Key features

- **It may be slow to thicken up** but regular pruning readily encourages plenty of fine branching.

- **Keep it out of frosts** and, if you are growing it indoors, away from direct heat. This is a tree that likes it not too hot and not too cold, but thrives in plenty of sunlight and humidity.

# Japanese elm
## *Zelkova serrata*

**If you are looking for a tough tree** that you can quickly grow into a small- or medium-sized specimen with a mass of fine branches, then zelkova is for you. Its autumn foliage is a bonus; it turns a deep yellow and is a wonderful sight. Zelkova is almost exclusively grown in the broom style, with its branches radiating out from roughly the same point on the trunk, like a broom. This mimics the shape of the tree when it grows in the wild.

### Key features

- **You can defoliate at least twice a year** in most climates to encourage very small leaves and dense branching. Remove any larger leaves as soon as possible.
- **Check regularly** for multiple branches growing from a single node and thin to no more than two branches.

Carry out directional pruning after the leaves have dropped off or been removed

Perfectly straight trunk

Planting the tree very slightly off-centre allows negative space to enhance the shape

In the broom style, all branches start from a similar point on the trunk and fan out

Root-prune with care to develop a well-rounded *nebari*

**25cm / 10in tall**
**Courtesy of Ian Cuppleditch**

### Looking closer

Top and centre: Fine branching is a feature of this tree. Prune the new growth back to a bud that is growing in the correct direction to encourage secondary and tertiary branches to develop. Below: The mass of fine branches is more obvious when the tree has shed its leaves in winter.

# Japanese maple
## *Acer palmatum* 'Deshojo'

**Think deciduous bonsai** and chances are you will picture an acer. There are several cultivars, each with a different growth habit and leaf type. The popular, elegant 'Deshojo' offers particularly fine red autumn foliage but is lovely at other times of year, too. Enjoy its spring bud break, its cooling green summer foliage, and its naked winter image – as well as its autumn colours.

### Key features

• **Young shoots and foliage can be tender** so protect them from wind and frost in spring until the leaves have hardened off.

• **To refine the branching,** create less length between the nodes. That means pinching out the central shoot between the opening leaves as soon as possible. Not fertilizing early in the year helps, too.

### Looking closer
Five-lobed leaves are especially vulnerable to damage caused by intense heat and wind. Defoliation reduces the size of the leaves and causes another burst of growth, but it also weakens the tree. You must be careful how much and how often you defoliate.

Aim to develop a shallow root system

Avoid over-dense branching by thinning out nodes with multiple branches

Bark turns brown or light grey with age

**90cm / 36in tall**
**Courtesy of Peter Chan**

# Flowering quince
## *Chaenomeles japonica*

**Normally in bloom from late winter to early spring,** in some climates, Japanese flowering quinces manage to produce their red, orangey-red, or white blooms (depending on the variety) almost all year round. In fact, this quince is known in Japanese as *Chojubai*, which translates as "long-living plum". But the flowering quince usually comes into its own in winter, when it presents a very striking image. This is the ideal choice if you are looking for a small-to-medium-sized flowering tree with winter interest.

### Key features

- **Fertilize, give plenty of water,** and provide a nutrient- and moisture-retentive soil for best results.

- **Add a little lava rock** when you transplant to improve aeration.

- **Always transplant** in autumn to reduce the risk of crown gall infection.

- **The bark turns flaky with age** but the trunk thickens slowly so you will need to be patient with it.

Defoliation encourages branching but do not defoliate more than once a year

**25cm / 10in tall**
Courtesy of John Brocklehurst

Beware of sharp little thorns

Wire the main branches into shape as soon as the leaves have hardened off

Poor health and excessive or strong fertilizer will make the leaves drop.

### Looking closer
Top: The quince's small leaves make it ideal for growing as a miniature *shohin* tree.
Centre: Remove the flowers as soon as they start to fade or they will form fruit and use all the plant's energy.
Below: Remove suckers from the base to keep the rootball neat.

# European hornbeam
## *Carpinus betulus*

**Hornbeams are deciduous woodland trees** that respond well to directional pruning and gentle corrective wiring, so you will easily be able to develop a natural-looking tree. They have superb autumn colouring too, ranging from yellow in the European hornbeam to the showy orange of the Korean variety. This colour combined with an attractive trunk – especially on older trees – makes for beautiful autumn and winter images.

## Key features

- **Encourage fine, delicate branching** by pruning the new spring growth back hard after the leaves have hardened off. You can do this year after year.

- **Strong, straight roots** that develop at the base of the trunk should be pruned back hard. They stunt the development of the finer branching roots that the tree needs for health.

### Looking closer
Top and below: Reduce the size of the leaves by giving less fertilizer in spring and by transplanting less often. Shade the leaves from strong sun. Centre: The attractive twin-trunk style was achieved by planting two trees close together.

The autumn foliage is a vibrant yellow

Fine branching is achieved by careful spring pruning

The elegant cascading style creates the impression of a windswept tree

Trunk texture and colour improve with age, giving added winter interest

The compact square pot restricts growth and gives a sense of stability

25cm / 10in tall
**Courtesy of Gavin Allen**

# Winged spindle
## *Euonymus alatus*

**The winged spindle or burning bush** gets its common names from the "wings" that develop on its branches and from its remarkable purplish-red leaves in autumn. In fact, there are other *Euonymus* species that are useful for bonsai, and all have superb autumn colours as well as flowers and fruit. A relatively easy tree to grow, the winged spindle responds well to pruning and will quickly develop into a lovely natural shape.

### Key features

- **Shaping is best achieved by pruning** as wiring risks damaging the "wings" on the branches.

- **Do not allow the soil to dry out** and make sure the leaves do not scorch in direct sunlight. It will also need protection from frost during winter.

The foliage of this burning bush is just turning red

Natural branching habit makes this an easy-to-shape tree

Still in its training pot, this tree can be moved to a smaller pot when you are happy with the way it has developed

Lower parts of the branches do not develop "wings" but gradually become corky

**30cm / 12in**
**Courtesy of Peter Warren**

### Looking closer

Above: If you want to use spindle as a *shohin* specimen you can reduce the size of the foliage by defoliation.

Centre and below: The difference between the bark of the stem and the winged bark is obvious. It is easier to bend the branches before they develop wings.

# Japanese holly
## *Ilex serrata*

**This deciduous tree really comes to life** from late autumn to spring, when you will see it laden with fruit. The combination of a thick trunk, well-proportioned branches, and tiny fruit is hard to beat. To get it to fruit you must have a large male tree to pollinate the female. That means only styling the female and leaving the male alone so it produces lots of branches with lots of flowers. The Japanese holly's attractive summer foliage is an added bonus.

### Key features

- **New growth** tends to grow vertically, which spoils the shape of the tree. Remove it in favour of lower growth and gently wire upward growth downwards to flatten it out.

- **This thirsty tree** likes a wet climate. Do not allow it to dry out when the fruit is setting.

- **Protect the fruit from birds** when the leaves drop or the birds will have a feast.

### Looking closer
Top: The small oval leaves are mid-green with a slightly rough texture and serrated edges.
Centre: If the tree dries out when it is setting fruit, the fruits will all drop off.
Below: The heavy base reveals scars where other trunks have been grown to develop thickness.

Do not defoliate if you want to have fruit

As the tree grows bigger, leaf size increases; limit this by pinching out new growth and restricting the amount of fertilizer in spring

To achieve a tapered upper trunk, first develop the thickness at the bottom, then encourage branching

A heavy base formed by a triple trunk is a typical style of growth for this tree

**52cm / 21in tall**
Courtesy of John Brocklehurst

# Amur maple
## *Acer ginnala*

**Some trees are outstanding** in one aspect of bonsai but not so good in others, and this is one of them. The undoubted star feature is its incredible autumn colour but it has slightly larger leaves and a less attractive growth habit than its more popular relatives, *A. palmatum* and *A. buergerianum*. It is much more difficult to encourage it to grow into a dense, well-branched tree, so it will always look less fetching in winter than its cousins. But that does not mean that we cannot appreciate it for what it does offer.

## Key features

- **Excelling for just two or three weeks a year** with lovely autumn foliage, in time the Amur maple also develops a very characterful trunk to admire year-round.

- **It has no special growing requirements.** Cultivate it the same way as you would *A. palmatum* (see p.74).

- **The lack of adventitious buds** is what makes it hard to grow this maple into an interesting shape.

Slightly large leaves and coarse tertiary branches

Trunk develops character with age

The *nebari* spreads widely across the surface

Intense yellow, orange, and red foliage in the autumn is the highlight of this species

Move it out of its training pot when a dense, compact root system has developed

**40cm / 16in tall**
**Courtesy of Mike Rose**

### Looking closer
Top: The tips of the branches tend to be slightly leggy and coarse.
Centre: After many years of cultivation in a pot, the trunk develops a subtle grey colour with attractive striations.
Below: Its autumn foliage is what makes this tree special.

# Blackthorn
## *Prunus spinosa*

**Every bonsai enthusiast should grow a *Prunus*.** It is a huge genus that includes plums, cherries, peaches, and almonds. This species, which is commonly known as blackthorn or sloe, is native to Europe and is particularly widespread in the UK. It has delicate, fragrant flowers, fruit (sloes), autumn colour, textured aged bark, and a naturally angular branch growth that is a wonder to behold and impossible to recreate with wire.

### Key features

- **Shape to achieve angular growth using** minimal wiring that pushes the branches in the desired direction. Then gently manipulate the secondary branches, ensuring that there is a straight line between each node.

- **These are fairly thirsty plants**, so make sure they do not dry out, especially during flowering if you want to have fruits. It is, however, best to remove fruits because they tire out the tree.

**Looking closer**
Above: The leaves have imperfections that add a very natural look to the tree.Centre and below: Distinctive cracked bark gives a sense of age and character that is impressive in winter.

**62cm / 24½in tall**
Courtesy of John Pitt

The delicate foliage turns red in autumn, then drops rather quickly

Regular pruning and defoliation will encourage branching but might reduce next year's flowers

Old wood and lignified branches are very hard but can be bent in midsummer

Strong surface roots are typical

The shallow pot accentuates the tree's size and proportions but means that the tree needs frequent watering

# Dwarf crab apple
## *Malus*

**If you want an easy-care fruiting tree** that is interesting in several seasons, then look no further than the *Malus* or crab apple genus. It will reward you with beautiful spring flowers followed by abundant fruit in autumn. The leaves can be a bit on the large side and the branch growth is very coarse, but those stunning flowers and fruit more than make up for the crab apple's defects.

**28cm / 11in tall**
Courtesy of John Pitt

## Key features

- **Growth is fast** but the branches will always be rather rounded and coarse and it is hard to get them to taper nicely.
- **Prune off any strong sucker-like** growth from old wood or the tree will suffer.
- **Fertilize heavily once the fruit has set** but do not fertilize during and just after flowering or the tree will focus on growing leaves rather than setting fruit.

Some of the fruit will stay on the tree in winter

Leaves are smaller on dwarf varieties

The trunk is cut back heavily when young to thicken it

Light-coloured pot accentuates the fruit and balances the heavy trunk

### Looking closer
Top and centre: Usually the flowers are pollinated naturally, but to be sure of successful fruiting, it is best to grow two or three different species of *Malus* close together.
Below: To achieve a thick characterful trunk, heavy cutting back over many years is needed.

# Japanese white beech
## *Fagus crenata*

**The remarkable feature of this deciduous tree** is the way its browned leaves stay on through winter and drop in spring. This is how it protects its buds during the coldest part of the year. The Japanese white beech also boasts a beautiful, smooth, silvery trunk. This combination of brown and silver provides a stunning winter image for bonsai enthusiasts to enjoy.

## Key features

- **Strong growth at the tips of the branches** and at the apex can block sunlight from the lower and internal branches. Regular pruning back to a weaker bud is the cure.

- **Unpruned roots become over-strong** and unbalanced. Root prune and transplant regularly to balance the growth of the roots.

**Looking closer**
Above and below: The tree has attractive wavy-edged leaves that are pale green in spring, glossy green in summer, and brown in autumn and winter. Centre: The tree's natural habit is to send out two very strong roots. Regular root-pruning will create a well-balanced *nebari*.

Brown winter foliage drops in spring when buds start to swell

Prune strong tips regularly to encourage tertiary branching

White trunk is a highlight if foliage is removed in the winter

Allow sunlight to reach the lower branches by regular pruning of the apex

**94cm / 37in tall**
Courtesy of Ian Cuppleditch

Shallow oval pot accentuates the tree's height and rounded silhouette

# English elm

## *Ulmus procera*

**Elms make excellent bonsai** and the English elm is especially good since its branches tend to be a little more lignified and less random than other elms. This tree's thick trunk and mass of fine growth at the tips of the branches make for a wonderful winter image. It is lovely in spring, too, when the vibrant green new leaves with their serrated edges make a striking contrast with the characterful ancient-looking trunk; a long-lived tree for all seasons.

### Key features

- **Do not allow** this tree to dry out but do not let it become waterlogged, either.

- **Being a native of northern,** temperate climates this tree can withstand the cold, but its long, flexible roots appreciate protection from hard frosts.

### Looking closer

Above and centre: The fissured, grey-brown trunk shows signs of *mochikomi*, the character that develops after many years' cultivation in a confined environment. Moss on the trunk adds to the tree's sense of age. Below: This old tree has a mass of tertiary branches.

The tertiary branches are delicate but well defined

Regularly thin dense areas and prune new shoots to create compactness

Trunk shows signs of age and *mochikomi*

The solid *nebari* suits this mature bonsai

**27cm / 11in tall**
**Courtesy of John Pitt**

Colour and rounded shape of the pot complement the winter image

# Local heroes

As bonsai has become more global it has gained a strong following in countries with very different climates. Not only has this introduced a variety of styles, species, and techniques, but the aesthetic is also very different, moving away from traditional Japanese conventions and styling and injecting the art form with fresh ideas and a new dynamism.

**Bonsai has always promoted the use of native trees:** how abstract or visually refined that native tree becomes is down to the aesthetic taste of the artist who creates it – and contrary to popular belief bonsai masters actively welcome the broadening of their art and practices. Any tree may be used for bonsai provided the fundamental principles are applied: an appreciation of nature, basic artistic design, and an understanding of the tree's underlying character and growth habit.

It would be contrary to those ideas to take a South African tree and style it in a classical Japanese way, so this section showcases some stars of the bonsai world that are very much more geographically specific.

Branches can become brittle within a few years so early wiring of young shoots is ideal

Branching shape created by wiring a basic skeleton structure

# Australian pine
## *Casuarina equisetifolia*

**With its needle-like evergreen foliage** and seeds similar to coniferous cones, this look-alike pine is found in India, Australasia, and South-east Asia, especially Indonesia. They can grow very fast and are nitrogen-fixing trees, so be cautious of excessive fertilizing. Shape with the clip-and-grow method and basic structural wiring.

### Key features

- **Although very drought resistant**, keep moist for best results. Due to symbiotic bacteria, some species enjoy being sprayed with salt water from time to time.
- **Feed with a low-nitrogen fertilizer** and regularly pinch out and remove dirty old needles, but never defoliate the tree.

With dedication delicate foliage can be pruned into compact foliage pads

Very well tapered trunk

Spreading surface roots give a sense of stability, important for a dynamic tree

**55cm / 22in tall**
**Courtesy of Mangala Rao**

Pot provides good balance and is the ideal size for hot, dry environments

### Looking closer
Top: Compact the needle-like foliage through regular pinching and pruning.
Centre and below: The *nebari* can be cultivated quite easily, and bark will start to show signs of age after a number of years of cultivation in a pot.

# Hawthorn
## *Crataegus monogyna*

**Although native throughout Europe,** the hawthorn is a particularly British tree and it is in Britain that you will find the best wild specimens. Choose it for its year-round interest – pretty foliage, lovely scented flowers and attractive fruits. As you might expect, it looks best when trained into a natural style.

### Looking closer
Above: The attractive fruits can last well into winter.
Centre: Leaves divided into between three and seven lobes are a dainty feature for bonsai.
Below: The hawthorn tends to flower when it is well settled in its pot, so you should avoid regular transplanting.

### Key features
- **Dead wood features,** including hollow trunks, are possible with hawthorn, but when working on a stump collected from the wild, avoid leaving carving marks.
- **Vigorous branches** can create dense, congested nodes. Regularly thin out nodes that have multiple branches growing from them.

From late autumn, protect fruit from bird damage

Foliage is generally small, making it good for bonsai

The trunk's *uro* feature adds character

Remove branches that grow up, down, or backwards to maintain a simple shape

The unglazed pot adds a sense of stability and strength that is ideal for this large, imposing tree

**104cm / 40in tall**
Courtesy of Ian Cuppleditch

# English oak

## *Quercus robur*

**The most quintessentially English of trees**, the oak conjures up images of strength, longevity, and the English countryside. This deep cultural resonance gives it meaning beyond its attractive shape. The oak's slightly large leaf size and the coarseness of its branches mean it is not as delicate a deciduous bonsai as, say, an acer, but it will reward you with superb autumnal colour.

### Key features

- **Deadwood features** such as staghorn-like *jins* and hollow trunks are viable options.

- **Best in a spreading upright style** but others are possible too.

- **You can decrease leaf size** by restricting root growth and giving less fertilizer in spring.

Work on ramification and to reduce leaf size requires patience

Good ventilation prevents mildew from attacking the leaves

Surface roots have developed into *nebari* as the tree has matured

Typical thick trunk for an oak

The slightly masculine pot balances the strong tree perfectly

**70cm / 28in tall**

**Courtesy of Harry Tomlinson**

### Looking closer

Above: The oakleaf shape is unmistakeable and the leaves can take on a wide range of colours throughout the year. Centre: The trunk's *uro* feature is an interesting character point. Below: Keep bark free of algae to avoid discoloration through lack of sunlight.

# Manila tamarind
## *Pithecellobium dulce*

**In some parts of the world** this prickly evergreen is regarded as invasive, but you can easily keep it under control as a bonsai. With its fast growth, long flowering period, edible fruit, and attractive spiral-shaped pods, it is a very rewarding plant. These examples have been cultivated as a group planting, creating the effect of a tropical forest in Mexico or Central America, the plant's region of origin.

### Key features

- **This fast-growing plant** tolerates severe pruning and can be pruned at any time of year. Mistakes quickly grow out. Pinching out stimulates branching.

- **Small white flowers appear** from November to May, followed by spiral, pinkish pods. The seeds are used in curries.

### Looking closer
Top and centre: Small, leathery evergreen leaves and compact branches are quick to develop in response to pruning. Below: The grey-brown trunks have a natural taper.

**50cm / 20in tall**
Courtesy of
Mangala Rao

This forest planting has an attractive rounded shape

Also known as Madras thorn, this plant can develop tiny spines

Exposed rootballs, moss, and tiny plants enhance the forest effect

Marble slab

# Lipstick ficus

## *Ficus virens* var. *glabella*

**If you name a plant after a type of cosmetic,** it will have a lot to live up to, and the lipstick fig does not disappoint. Its soft new leaves are a spectacular bright pink with cream-coloured veins. They change to lime-green then become stiffer, darker green leaves in just a few days. This is a bold, large-leaved plant, so do not expect to cultivate a small, delicate bonsai.

### Key features

- **This tropical tree** is a fast grower so it needs constant work to develop it effectively. You can grow it into any style except broom style.

- **Frequent pruning** will lead to slightly more compact growth and slightly smaller leaves. It buds readily from older wood.

Handsome, stiff mature leaves

Like all figs, this variety has a well-defined trunk

Root restriction prevents the growth of aerial roots that characterize the tree in the wild

The shallow rounded pot balances the tall, rounded growth

70cm / 28in tall

**Courtesy of Mangala Rao**

### Looking closer

Top: The stunning new leaves appear after a very brief period of leaf fall.
Centre: Trunk and branches will quickly develop an aged appearance.
Below: The fruits are small, smooth, and greenish, with tiny red dots when ripe.

# California juniper
## *Juniperus californica*

**As its name suggests,** this juniper is native to California, where it tolerates extreme drought and heat. This particular example was collected in the Mojave Desert. *Yamadori* of this quality are rare these days. Although they grow slowly in arid conditions, they will thrive with proper fertilizer and water.

### Key features

- **California junipers** are often found to have very small live veins compared to the amount of dead wood – testament to their powers of survival.

- **Dead wood is hard and durable** but ensure it does not start to rot when it is in daily contact with water.

### Looking closer
Top and below: Sinuous, aged and weathered wood is a desirable feature, sometimes found on *yamadori*.
Centre: California junipers have coarse foliage to combat the arid conditions, but it can be compacted over time.

Use wire to guide the growing branches gently in the desired direction

Hard, durable dead wood

Recently styled foliage pads are yet to bulk up to their full density

Strong yet feminine pot complements the elegant and not overly dramatic nature of the tree

**90cm / 36in tall**
**Courtesy of Ryan Neil**

# Coastal redwood
## Sequoia sempervirens

A species renowned for its height and straightness as well as its ability to regenerate and regrow, collected material from second and third growth forests along the Californian coast make ideal bonsai specimens. They prefer moist climates and enjoy semi shade in summer and protection in winter. Their growth habit means that many adventitious shoots sprout from the trunk; with care and effort, foliage pads can be created.

## Key features
- **The dead wood features** are entirely natural, and stunted second growth trees are created by natural forces as well as commercial forestry.
- **The delicate leaves** will burn in hot sun and also drop in very cold winters, so protect from extreme conditions.

Now the basic skeleton structure has been created, in a few years dense foliage pads will form with careful pruning

Foliage is fine, compact, and similar in appearance to *Taxus*

### Looking closer
Top and below: One of the beauties of *yamadori* trees is their natural character. Avoid carving for the sake of it and try to leave the feature as natural as possible unless the design requires it.
Centre: Dense foliage pads are created by selective pruning.

Redwood trunks offer great possibilities for carving

**52cm / 21in tall**
**Courtesy of Ryan Neil**

Strong masculine pot, ideal for the visually heavy tree it contains

# Rocky Mountain juniper
## *Juniperus scopulorum*

**Found mainly along the Rocky Mountains**, this juniper is renowned for its ability to grow and survive in extreme conditions, which give rise to the incredible dead wood features. The foliage is delicate and fine in comparison to the California juniper and will soon turn juvenile if pruned excessively.

### Key features

- **As with all junipers,** the trick is to constantly keep it growing whilst still pruning back to maintain vigour and stop juvenile foliage being produced.

- **Fine foliage varieties** are susceptible to damage. Keep an eye out for tip blight during the growing season.

**90cm / 36in tall**
Courtesy of Ryan Neil

### Looking closer
Top and below: The natural dead wood has outstanding character which cannot be replicated by the hand of man. Hard and durable, it speaks volumes about the struggles the tree has endured.
Centre: Dense branching is achieved by ramification.

Naturally formed dead wood offers a contrast to the fine foliage

Dead wood features are just as they were found in the wild

Prune the new growth whilst leaving strong growing tips to continue on a regular basis

Subtle colour and texture of the wood-fired pot complements the tree

# Ponderosa pine
## *Pinus ponderosa*

**Found on mountain slopes**, high mesas, and dry valleys, the ponderosa pine tolerates wind, drought, poor soil, and low winter temperatures. The contorted natural shapes are a testament to this pine's ability to endure and be flexible yet strong – and the combination of pliable branches and adventitious budding make it an ideal candidate for bonsai.

### Key features

- **Work on ramification** and give plenty of sun to encourage branching and shorten needle growth.

- **Reducing the number of needles** on strong areas and leaving weaker areas untouched will help to redistribute energy. Do not candle cut this pine: remove strong terminal buds from vigorous areas where adventitious buds already exist.

Pruning the strong terminal buds encourages adventious buds to form and strengthen

A natural formed *jin* where a branch has snapped off

The natural movement of the trunk is all but impossible to recreate with a non collected tree

The trunk has a good natural taper

For optimum health, repot with a little of the original, native soil

### Looking closer
Top and below: Craggy, contorted bark is a key feature.
Centre: Clusters of buds form at the tip of last year's growth. They will develop into candles and then into whorls of shoots.

**80cm / 32in tall**

**Courtesy of Ryan Neil**

# Dramatic effects

Many varieties used in bonsai occur naturally in the harshest environments and some of the finest specimens have been collected from the wild to exploit the age and characteristics imbued by a tough existence. Successfully combining the great character found in an established trunk with man-made styling of branches and foliage pads is the bonsai artist's ultimate challenge.

**Material collected from the wild** is known as *yamadori* and it is the source of a vast number of masterpiece bonsai across the world. The ethics of collecting are down to the individual, but it should never be seen as an unlimited source of free material and trees must only be taken at the correct time of year to ensure success. It goes without saying that in most countries you cannot just go out and dig up material; trees must be legal to collect, and permission must always be obtained first. There may be powerful environmental reasons for leaving a tree where it grows. Excessive, illegal collection combined with poor survival rates due to lack of aftercare are a huge problem so if you long to own one of these very special trees, it is recommended that you buy collected material from a reputable bonsai nursery.

This tree has only been wired once since collection; foliage pads and branches are yet to be refined

Cascading nature of tree starts with the roots and finishes in the well-balanced foliage pad

# Mountain pine

## *Pinus mugo*

**The tough, rugged European pine** is a superb species for bonsai with flexible branches that withstand dramatic transformations and textured bark that develops with age. It readily sends out adventitious buds; with increased ramification and prolonged cultivation, the length of its needles can be reduced. Compact the foliage pads by regular pruning to create a very mature-looking tree.

Dead wood feature left as nature intended

### Key features

- **Needles can be thick and fleshy**, so take care to avoid congested buds. Thin out strong terminal growth to promote adventitious buds.

- **Thin out needles** only where definition between branches is required, or if they are dirty. New buds are likely to form at the base of old needles.

Deep textured pot is on the large side to accommodate the root system – often a factor with collected trees

**35cm / 14in tall**
**Courtesy of John Pitt**

### Looking closer

Top: With careful management the needle size may be reduced.
Centre: Thick strong roots hold the cascade in position.
Below: The dead wood feature is left as it was found: natural character often tops anything man-made so think twice before you work on such features.

# European larch
## *Larix decidua*

A *tenjin* at the top suggests a tree that has survived a harsh environment

**This European *yamadori* larch is nothing if not dramatic.** It was collected from the Italian Alps. Larches do not appreciate root-pruning so this specimen, with its well-established root system, presented quite a challenge. Clearly a traditional pot would not do. The owner, who also created the pot and the stand, came up with this inventive and artistic solution. You sometimes have to think out of the box – or pot!

60cm / 24in tall

Courtesy of John Pitt

Slightly less coarse growth than Japanese larch

### Looking closer

Top: Natural, grasping roots made this an ideal candidate for a semi-cascade tree.
Centre: The delicate foliage is arranged in whorls. Pale green in spring and summer, it turns golden yellow in autumn.
Below: The textured pot complements the gnarled trunk.

The unique spherical rock-textured pot was created specially for this tree by John Pitt

A dramatic, cascading branch adds movement and direction to the composition

### Key features

- **As the tree ages,** it can develop superb bark, distinguished by characterful ridges and cracks.

- **Growth is less coarse** than in Japanese larch but you can minimise coarseness by regular thinning. In general, this species has delicate branches.

- **The larch is a vigorous grower.** It can replace pruned growth extremely quickly.

# Olive
## *Olea europea* var. *sylvestris*

The dead wood *tenjin* provides a counterpoint to the compact foliage

**Living hundreds of years in the wild,** olives are tough, resilient trees and respond well to training. This small-leaved variant, like its larger-leaved cousin, is often used for bonsai, and to dramatic effect. Collected specimens such as this often have very interesting dead wood features. Add aged flaky bark, tiny leaves, and compact branching, and this example packs a punch.

*Shari* on the trunk adds age, drama, and character

Tight foliage pads created by regular pruning to shape

Take care not to damage the old, flaky bark

A solid base is essential for a thin, elegant *literati*

**50cm / 20in tall**
**Courtesy of Mike Rose**

**Looking closer**
Top: This tiny-leaved variety comes from parts of Spain, and especially from Majorca. The leaves persist in winter.
Centre and below: The dead wood is exactly as it was found; it has only been cleaned. Using tools on it would introduce a sense of the artificial.

## Key features

- **The live wood and the dead wood** are similar in colour so, unlike junipers or *Taxus*, the contrast is not as stark. Work to ensure that the subtle difference is maintained and the line between the two is defined.

- **The leaves are naturally small** but they can be reduced further by defoliation and by restricting the amount of fertilizer.

The tiny pot suggests a harsh environment, yet the viewer does not fear the tree will fall over

# Sabina juniper
## *Juniperus sabina*

**This juniper is yet another example** of the ever-popular juniper family. Common to many parts of Europe, they are occasionally collected from the wild, which is where this example started its bonsai life.
It gives a wonderfully aged and dramatic impression.

Dead wood features are a result of the harsh mountainous conditions

Branches need to be wired to point the foliage towards the sun for success

Live vein twists around the lower trunk in typical juniper fashion

55cm / 22in tall
**Courtesy of Peter Chan**

## Looking closer
Top and centre: The branches have been carefully manipulated to continue the appearance of age.
Below: The foliage will become dense with correct management but has a tendency to become quite flat or downward pointing.

## Key features

- **Foliage management** is essential: ensure it points upwards for full strength, and remove any that has flowered to stimulate new growth.

- **Dead wood is soft**; clean out rotten wood and use a hardening product on areas in contact with soil.

# Tamarisk

## *Tamarix chinensis*

**Graceful feathery foliage and dangling plume-like pink flowers** in spring and summer mark the tamarisk out as a shrub to watch. It suits a weeping style, but needs a certain amount of encouragement as it naturally wants to grow upward. Although they look dainty, tamarisks are coastal plants and resist salt and wind; in fact, they positively thrive in a windy spot. Enjoy seeing their branches shimmer in even the slightest breeze.

Branches gracefully curve down naturally under their own weight in the wild

Dead wood contrasts with the live veins

The old stump that was the starting point has been beautfully carved

85cm / 34in tall

Carved and styled by Hotsumi Terakawa

A small, shallow container restricts the tree's growth

## Key features

- **To counteract** the tamarisk's natural upward growth habit, wire the new growth gently downwards before it has had a chance to become too hard to bend.

- *Yamadori* **are relatively rare** but offer the possibility of incredible dead wood features.

**Looking closer**
Top: Plume-like spring flowers underline the plant's airy quality.
Centre: Slender, drooping branches are covered in scale-like foliage.
Below: The trunk has been carved and has a dramatic, two-tone effect.

# Creating
## your own
# Bonsai

All the skills and techniques you need to execute your own designs – whether instant keshiki, tumbling cascades, or dramatic rock planting displays.

# Looking after your first bonsai

A popular first tree, Chinese elms soon grow out of shape. Do not be afraid to prune back or remove branches – ultimately you will improve the tree.

**The finished tree, restyled and repotted**

### The secret shape
Attacking your first tree may be a daunting prospect: the trick is to be clear about your aim. Here the idea is to create a more rounded broom-like silhouette, broadly triangular in shape.

Until now this elm has been grown by topiary pruning, and a number of unnecessary branches are still on the tree

Long, leggy growth is all over the tree

Dead tertiary branches on the inside

Renew the poor soil as soon as possible – and consider choosing a more attractive pot

### Assess your tree
Left for just a month, shoots grow wild, and unbalanced growth develops as strong areas become stronger and weaker ones weaken further. It is imperative to address this as soon as possible, and it's also an opportunity to make structural improvements.

# Create a strong framework

1 **Remove the dead branches** to get a better idea of what you can use to create the tree. Dead twigs will snap off easily in your fingers, just by rubbing them.

2 **Use pruners** to take out the larger dead shoots. Branches die off if they don't get the right combination of water, light, and fertilizer; thinning out crowded areas can help to strengthen your tree just by letting in more light. Weak branches may also die if stronger ones are allowed to dominate, so aim to prevent this happening in future.

3 **Remove any unsightly branches**. This includes shoots growing back into the centre of the tree, and those that grow directly upwards or that are too straight. Also look at any areas where more than two branches emerge from the same junction (node), and simplify the complicated structure. Imagine an idealized branching structure, and work towards achieving it.

4 **Without the unnecessary branches**, your tree should look a lot better, with a much more powerful structure. When pruning bonsai, always start by creating a strong framework before you tackle vigorous leggy growth: if you accidentally take off the wrong branch, young flexible shoots may be repositioned with wire to fill any gaps in your design.

Nodes with more than two branches are radically thinned

Make sure the main framework is set before attacking the straggly growth

# Trim into shape: clip and grow

Mark the best front view and stand back now and again to check your work from this angle

6 **Prune back** to a bud that will grow in the right direction and fill space; also include a change from the current direction. Allow a short distance between each change of direction, usually no more than two leaves.

5 **Prune to shape**. Reduce branches extending out of the silhouette; ensure they have leaves – or visible buds – before you prune back to just above the first leaf joint. This encourages new shoots to grow, especially if you defoliate the tree once the leaves have hardened off (see p.127).

**The clip-and-grow method (directional pruning)** is ideal for Chinese elms. Once pruned back, the branch will grow out in the direction of the terminal bud which is pointing off at an angle.

7 **Treat all the cut areas** with wound sealant (see pp.108–109). If it is a suitable time of year, consider transplanting the tree (see pp.129–133). Improving the style and quality of the pot will give you a lot more enjoyment, so look for a better pot combination.

"*The finished tree has an open, graceful structure on which new growth can be built*"

**The repotted tree has a more individual image**. The subtle colour and rounded edges of the rectangular pot add a sense of grace and femininity to the composition – ideal for deciduous trees. The planting position and slight change of angle add negative space on the right, which makes for a more artistic and dynamic feel.

# Designing a deciduous tree

For the best results when styling bonsai, always consider the species and natural growth habit of the material. With just a few basic concepts and techniques you can create unique designs every time.

## Choosing suitable trees

Look for a tree with an attractive trunk line that tapers nicely, with few visible scars. The branches should have an initial upward movement and be well balanced in thickness, length, angle, and position. Check the *nebari* (root flare) under the soil surface.

- **Best trees** include maples, hornbeams, stewartia (used here), elms, and beech.
- **Consider the leaves** and their impact on the design. You may be able to reduce the leaf size on some species.

**The restyled tree three months later**

# Plan your design

1 **Examine the tree** from all angles to choose the front view. Most deciduous trees have three points that are almost impossible to correct: the *nebari*, the shape or movement in the lower trunk, and the position of the branches. The best front and design will balance all these factors.

**Branches** coming from the same node or very close to each other can be reduced down to the best-placed and most interesting shoots. Try covering the branches in turn to see how the tree would look without the branch – once a branch has been cut off, it cannot be replaced.

**Mark the front of the tree** when you have found the best trunk line and decided which branches to remove.

1

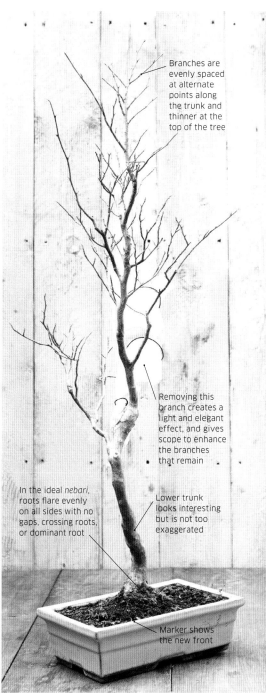

Branches are evenly spaced at alternate points along the trunk and thinner at the top of the tree

Removing this branch creates a light and elegant effect, and gives scope to enhance the branches that remain

In the ideal *nebari*, roots flare evenly on all sides with no gaps, crossing roots, or dominant root

Lower trunk looks interesting but is not too exaggerated

Marker shows the new front

# Making cuts and sealing wounds

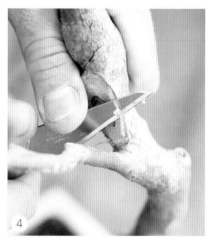

**Use a small-toothed saw** to remove any branches larger than pencil thickness. Removing large branches can cause dieback, but the branch directly below the wound ensures this is not a concern.

**Keep cuts as small as possible**, but the priority is to ensure wounds can heal in an attractive way. By making a slightly larger cut flush to the trunk this scar will become almost invisible in future.

**Shave off the rough edges** of the wound using a sharp, sterile knife, and shape so that it is completely flush to the trunk. This speeds up the callusing process and ensures the final scar is less intrusive.

# Improving shape and taper

**Prune the remaining branches** into shape. Here the aim is to introduce a natural-looking change of direction by encouraging upwards and outwards growth, and create a tapered shape.

**To encourage compact branching** and introduce natural changes of direction, look at reducing straight sections. Most deciduous trees produce more secondary branching when pruned to healthy buds.

5

**When the cut stops bleeding**, apply a thin layer of suitable wound sealant, such as paste containing antifungal and antibacterial agents. Use it sparingly: a thick cake can actually inhibit healing.

6

Over time, the seal degrades and falls off

**Allow the sealant to dry.** The seal will stay on the tree for several years until the callus forms naturally underneath. Don't be tempted to remove the sealant to see what is happening beneath it.

7

**For larger wounds**, especially on species such as *Stewartia* that are very slow to callus, you may want to apply sticky-backed aluminium tape over the top of the wound to promote rapid healing.

New leader

Remove the old dominant shoot (leader)

10

**The taper** can often be improved by pruning back the trunk to create a new leader. In this case the new leading shoot will continue growing to the left, enhancing the tree's overall direction.

The new leader gives the tree a delicate tapered shape and introduces movement to the left

11

**After pruning** the new apex should be more defined, and the overall structure of the tree much clearer. After wiring the tree may be pruned a little more to finish off the shape.

## How to wire the trunk

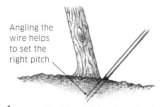

Angling the wire helps to set the right pitch

1 **Use suitably thick wire.** Push one end deep into the soil as close to the trunk as possible. Avoid damaging the *nebari* or sub-surface roots.

2 **Bend the wire around the trunk** starting from the base. Make sure it is in contact with the trunk; don't leave any gaps or straight sections.

3 **Continue the wire up the trunk.** Check that the coils are evenly spaced and pitched consistently at a 45–55° angle.

4 **For extra strength** when making severe bends add a second wire. On conifers place wires next to each other and keep together up the tree.

# Wiring explained

Wiring is the bonsai artist's paintbrush: it allows you to manipulate the trunk, branches, and foliage at will. The wire brace must be safe, effective, and ideally unobtrusive so that you can bend a branch without it snapping and hold it in the new position until it sets.

## Getting started

Always consider which direction the branch is going to be bent, and where the bend will be. The wire must always be on the outside of the curve so that it acts as a brace against snapping. Here the branch is to bend downwards from the base.

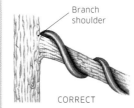

Branch shoulder

CORRECT

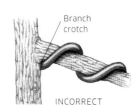

Branch crotch

INCORRECT

LINKING BRANCHES

**Work from the centre of the wire out**, and start on the branch "shoulder". Make sure the wire sits close to the trunk without any gaps. When the branch tries to return to its original position after bending, the wire will be in the way holding it in place.

**If on a downward bend** the wire starts at the branch "crotch", when bending is attempted the wire will act as a pivot and encourage the branch to break: there is nothing to stop the top part of the branch tearing away from the trunk or snapping.

**It is always preferable** to wire two branches with a single length of wire – here they are separated by a section of trunk which also acts as an anchor. Both of these branches can be lowered because the wires on each one go over the shoulder.

## Which kind of wire?

Two types are used: annealed copper, and anodised aluminium wire (*see p.39*). The key difference is the holding strength offered against the diameter of the wire – a 2mm copper wire offers roughly the same ability to bend and hold as a 4mm aluminium wire.

As a general rule use copper for conifers: the wires may stay on the tree up to three years, depending on vigour. Wire brittle deciduous trees and azaleas with aluminium: their bark is more easily damaged and generally the wires will need removing within a few months.

## How to wire a branch

If an entire branch is wired, wire secondary branches in pairs with anchorage in between – usually a thicker wire along the main branch. Always make sure you anchor the wires to increase stability, otherwise when one branch is bent, its pair can move or return to its original position.

ORIGINAL BRANCH

1 **Wire the primary branch.** With a thick wire – connected to either the trunk or to a nearby thick branch – apply wire along the main line. With practice and experience you'll be able to plan the pairs of secondary branches to be wired together and position the main wire accordingly, so that secondary wires can be applied easily and effectively.

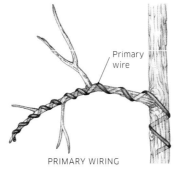

Primary wire

PRIMARY WIRING

2 **Wire secondary branches** of similar thickness together with a medium-sized wire. This second wire should run alongside the "primary" wire for one complete coil and then flow naturally on to the secondary branch. Ideally the two wires should never cross.

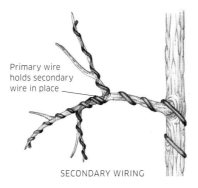

Primary wire holds secondary wire in place

SECONDARY WIRING

3 **Wire tertiary branches** and smaller secondary branches at the tip using thin wire. In each case wire connects two branches with an anchor point of larger gauge wire between them. It is best not to have more than two wires running alongside each other, but sometimes this is unavoidable. Each branch can now be independently manipulated into position.

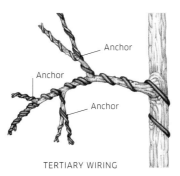

Anchor

Anchor

Anchor

TERTIARY WIRING

## Heavy wiring techniques

For major manipulation multiple wires may be needed. Ideally run the wires in tandem, but on brittle trees keep them separate to increase the surface area that prevents the branch snapping. It is untidy, but effective – and on these trees wire is soon removed.

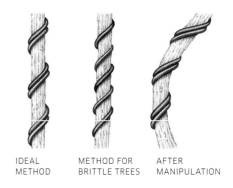

IDEAL METHOD

METHOD FOR BRITTLE TREES

AFTER MANIPULATION

## Wiring the whole tree

The diagram shows how to wire the trunk and primary branches of an entire tree for its first styling. Note that one of the main trunk wires stops halfway up at the point where just one wire is enough to bend the trunk. None of the wires cross: they all run parallel to the existing wire.

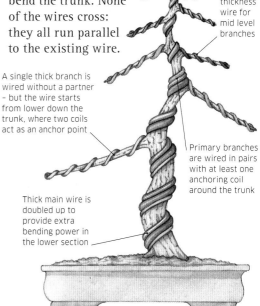

Medium thickness wire for mid level branches

Primary branches are wired in pairs with at least one anchoring coil around the trunk

A single thick branch is wired without a partner – but the wire starts from lower down the trunk, where two coils act as an anchor point

Thick main wire is doubled up to provide extra bending power in the lower section

# Wiring to shape

12 **Wire the branches** that need to be moved, starting with the thickest. Aim to wire branches in pairs with a single length of wire. Start at the base of the lowest branch. Loop the wire around the tree, ensuring both ends are long enough to wire the two branches, and hold it securely against the trunk with one hand – your anchor hand.

Anchor hand holds wire firmly in place

Wiring hand

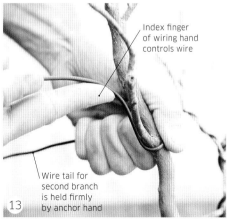

Index finger of wiring hand controls wire

Wire tail for second branch is held firmly by anchor hand

13 **Apply gentle pressure** with the index finger of your other "wiring" hand to guide and rotate the wire around the lowest branch. Ensure the wire sits comfortably on top of the branch: it should neither float above it with visible gaps, nor be so tight that it digs into the bark.

Anchor hand stays still until both ends of wire are locked around the branches

14 **Lock the wire in place** by completing one full rotation around the first branch. Keep your anchor hand firmly in position as your wiring hand switches to the tail end of the wire and rotates it around the second branch.

15 **With both wires locked,** tackle each branch separately. Use your wiring hand to wrap each shoot, and the anchor to support the branches behind the wire, preventing the loops pulling too tight, and moving branches out of the way.

Wind the wire evenly around each branch at 45° angles

16 **Gently shape the tree**. Deciduous trees are brittle, so only introduce slight movement and avoid making exaggerated curves.

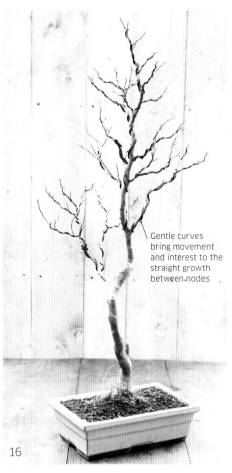

Gentle curves bring movement and interest to the straight growth between nodes

# Styling a young juniper

Flexible and easy to care for, junipers are a popular choice for bonsai as they can be quickly transformed into interesting trees. They live in the harshest environments, so dynamic trees are both possible and desirable.

Vigorous stems offer plenty of scope for manipulation

The deep green foliage and light green tips are a sign of perfect health

Internal foliage is a healthy dark green colour

Twin trunks with strong movement to one side are balanced in size and foliage mass

## Choosing suitable trees

There are a number of junipers that suit bonsai cultivation – but many garden species are much less suitable. For best results choose one of the compact foliage types, such as the Chinese juniper (*Juniperus chinensis*) shown here. The trunk and branches can be bent dramatically with ease when young – and using more advanced techniques when old – so it is possible to change the structure.

- **Branches** with long, thin extensions and plenty of foliage are a sign of strong, vigorous growth.
- **Foliage** should be deep green with light green growing tips. Junipers can suffer from spider mite damage or tip blight so check the internal foliage and branch tips for health.
- **Trunk** Look for dramatic movement, and perhaps interesting dead wood.

# Create the main structure

1 **Clear the base.** Here the small lower shoots on both main trunks are removed. Wire the trunk and main branches using a suitably heavy gauge copper wire.

2 **Manipulate the trunk.** It can be bent dramatically – in this case initially down and away from the front, then back up and towards the front in a slightly higher position.

3 **Create the shape.** On this tree one branch is bent quite sharply down from the base to make the branch on the left-hand side. If the base of a branch splits or tears, treat the wound immediately with wound sealant.

4 **Refine the movement.** Bend the branches left and right as well as down and up to create movement in the horizontal and vertical planes. The goal is to compact the branch and create a voluminous foliage pad from secondary branches.

5 **Finish the structure.** Here the aim is a windswept twin trunk image – so the space between the two trunks is important as well as dramatic movement towards the right.

6 **Junipers are very flexible** and when wired correctly with suitably thick copper wire, the introduction of dramatic bends like this is not a problem at all.

Shape the branch with a series of fluid curves in all directions

Double copper wires used for extra flexibility

Wires are firmly anchored deep in the soil

# Fine-tuning the foliage pads

7 **Wire secondary branches** once the main structure is set. Do not prune off any tertiary branches at this stage because the final orientation may not yet be fixed.

8 **Manipulate the branches**. Shape each secondary shoot in a similar way to the main branch – left and right, as well as up and down. Do not create an unnatural pig tail effect: the ideal curve allows the shoot to fan out naturally on the outside of a bend, or top of the branch.

9 **Prune secondary shoots** coming from the inside of a curve, or that are growing downwards – but if a branch is very bare, retain some of the better placed shoots.

10 **Leave the remaining shoots unpruned**. It is vital that the growing tips are left intact and allowed to grow. They will be pruned back in future but for now they are needed to power the tree forwards and help it recover from this transformation.

**Over time**
• The tiny shoots will grow out and fill in the space without needing to be wired.
• The foliage pad may be pruned and cleaned into a rough shape; only minor fine wiring will be necessary.
• On the first styling very little fine work is done. Once the major branches are set, refinement can continue.

_"The finished tree has restful areas of negative space and a graceful rhythm"_

## Managing juniper foliage

Remove fruits to divert energy into foliage

**Junipers gain strength** from active, healthy foliage; if this is dramatically reduced, the shock induces undesirable needle-like juvenile growth. Never remove more than 40 per cent of foliage at one time, and ensure that the remaining foliage has active light green growing tips.

**Increase adventitious budding** by pruning a terminal growth tip only if there are several more behind it that will race to take its place as the terminal bud.

**Clean out internal foliage** with no active tips, often due to flowering in the past. Removing them and pruning the terminal tip will stimulate adventitious growth.

# Styling an upright maple

Deciduous trees take years to develop: a cycle of growing out, then pruning back hard introduces thickness, taper, and natural changes of direction. It can be daunting, but on this maple you can see how the initial styling is done.

## Assess your tree

Look for interesting lines: they may already exist, or they can be created by the removal of undesirable lines. This 'Deshojo' maple has two strong lines coming from a central point that creates a twin trunk feel – a typical feature of deciduous trees – even though it is halfway up the tree.

Ignore the tips of long, leggy branches and consider the position, angle, and thickness of the node on the lower part of the branch

The strongest line in the apex moves to the right, away from the second "trunk" on the left

The second "trunk" has a couple of strong branches which have only a few secondary shoots

The nebari is very well balanced for a tree of this heritage; always check before purchase or starting work

**Field-grown material** like this maple should be undercut every other year (as this tree has been) to develop compact roots, and roughly branch pruned at regular intervals. It has grown freely in the pot for 18 months to put on roots and allow the branches to thicken.

# Create the basic framework

1 **Reduce the apex** to remove straightness in the upper section and most importantly introduce taper into the top section. Prune back to a node with several well-placed and very strong branches using a saw to ensure a clean and accurate cut.

2 **Choose the new front.** Here the new angle is based on the best relationship between the primary trunk and the very strong main branch – the *nebari* is a neutral factor because it shows even growth all around the base. Remove whippy lower branches from the trunk and cut back long branches to a junction with a suitable secondary shoot.

3 **Thin out multiple branches** removing weak growth and shoots growing in the wrong direction until only two branches are left from each node (*see also p.120*). This is a fundamental concept for deciduous trees. Always prune back to a point just above a strong branch or bud on a node.

4 **Defoliate the branches** after pruning. This tree was pruned in autumn on the cusp of leaf drop – the best time for deciduous trees – so foliage was removed after the majority of the stored starches had been transported back into the tree.

Scar from a previous reduction in height

Primary trunk
Secondary trunk

Remove the leaves to show the structure

# Thinning congested nodes

Mass of young shoots caused by pruning a major branch

Aim to keep just two strong branches, to create the main and secondary lines

Third branch

First major branch

Second branch is a vigorous young shoot

6

Third branch

First branch

Second branch

7

Keeping the downward shoot helps improve the line and taper of the main branch

8

**Assess congested nodes.** Young or very vigorous trees such as maples typically respond to pruning by sending out a mass of new shoots below the pruned area. Often multiple buds spring from a single node; if they are left to develop it can cause "inverse taper", in which the small section of the branch where all the secondary shoots are growing becomes thicker than the branch below it.

6 **Select the shoots to retain.** Here, close examination reveals three strong branches – two green older ones, and a vigorous red shoot – as well as several medium and weaker shoots, all of which can be removed.

7 **Assess the node again.** With the unwanted shoots out of the way it is easier to decide which shoots to keep. On this example, the third branch appears to be growing in towards the main trunk, so it is pruned out.

**Check the line and prune if necessary.** Here, an attractive line and branch pairing has been created; the main branches will be defoliated and then reduced to a more suitable length before they are wired. Don't prune too hard at this stage: it is easier to bend a long branch than a short one, and the tree can be pruned again after manipulation.

# Making heavy bends on deciduous trees

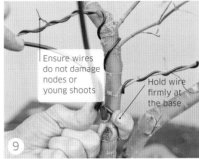

Ensure wires do not damage nodes or young shoots

Hold wire firmly at the base

**Wire the branches**. When planning dramatic movement always make sure wire is positioned on the back of the branch where the bend is desired.

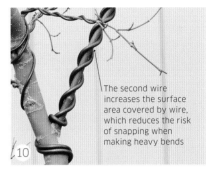

The second wire increases the surface area covered by wire, which reduces the risk of snapping when making heavy bends

**Wire the shoot again for extra support.** Keep the same angle but wrap the second wire in the centre of the gap between the existing coils.

Anchor hand

**Bend the branch.** This is a two-handed, ten-fingered operation. Use your anchor hand to secure the base of the branch and define the pivot point. With your other hand, apply even pressure to the branch in small massaging movements.

The shoots at the end are left here to grow but may be reduced once it has set in place

The branch now curves upwards and then sharply down, introducing movement and interest to the tree

**Keep an eye on the wire.** Branches with dramatic bends will push hard against the wire trying to return to the original position, so are more prone to injury. Remove wires immediately if they appear to bite into the bark.

# Refining an azalea

A combination of late spring/early summer flowers, small leaves, and an ability to bud on old wood make Satsuki azaleas a popular choice for bonsai. They can be very brittle and have a different growth habit that requires some special techniques for success.

**The finished tree, six months later**

*Hoshi no Kagayaki.* Small star-shaped flowers are almost spent and need to be removed

## Special points for Satsuki

Success with azaleas is often more of a horticultural challenge: they demand a particular, slightly more acidic pH of soil and water, and keeping them well-fed, well-watered, and pest free can be difficult in the hot summer months. Left to their own devices, Satsuki azaleas are multi-stemmed clump-forming shrubs. In bonsai they are usually styled into artificial classical or abstract shapes that are very different from their natural habit – any styling is possible, just keep it coherent and attractive.

• **New growth** needs to be significantly thinned: this can mean reducing four or more new stems to just two shoots.
• **Tertiary branches** require hard pruning every few years to ensure the branch tips do not become too old and woody (lignified). Satsuki readily bud on old wood so healthy plants generally recover from a defoliation and branch pruning.

# Remove the spent flowers

1 **Remove the flowers** as soon as their petals start to wilt. If wilted petals get wet there is a high probability of fungal problems developing, so act promptly and remove the whole bloom – both the purple petals and the central ovular stem. If the ovule is left to develop it will turn to seed and the tree will become exhausted.

2 **Hold the branch steady** with one hand just behind the tip, then pinch and twist off the petals and the central ovule. Take care not to pull too hard to avoid damaging the branch.

3 **Foliage** remains at the end of the branch, but the flower is removed entirely. From this point you can expect at least two – and perhaps four or five – new shoots to develop within about two weeks.

4 **With the flowers removed** it is time to start thinking about the styling of your azalea. This example has grown out of shape: there are a number of leggy branches, and the structure lacks definition.

Long leggy growth will need to be tackled

# Create the basic skeleton

Start by removing the weakest stems and spindly growth

5

**Thin out congested trunks.** This azalea has an unsightly clump of six or seven stems originating from a single node near the base of the second trunk, which needs to be reduced down to just two.

6

**Carefully remove the weakest growth** with branch cutters. Gradually thin out the clump, continually assessing the tree's overall structure until just two strong, well-positioned stems remain.

Clean the wound and cover with sealant

7

**Treat the wound** (*see pp.108–109*). The scar will form a small callus that will eventually become less obvious. The thinned tree now has a pleasing branch division with a natural looking V-shape.

Six shoots from one node grow in all directions

8

**Thin out crowded branch tips.** It may be difficult to decide which are the best placed pair; always remove branches growing directly up or down, back into the tree, or any that are very strong.

Two horizontal branches create a clear framework

9

**Horizontal branches** can help to create a good structural skeleton. Here, the shoots that remain are relatively thin, but they are nicely placed and separate in a pleasing, well-balanced V-shape.

# Wire and shape the tree

**Azaleas are particularly brittle** but may be shaped when young. Use aluminium wire and for extra security choose a slightly thicker gauge than normal.

**Double wire thicker branches** to allow more movement to be introduced. Wire branches in pairs using both hands, and ensure the wires are securely anchored.

**Thinner branches can also be wired** but are easy to snap as you work. Satsuki respond to pruning – so to avoid delicate wiring, clip and grow them into shape.

**Wire secondary and tertiary branches in pairs.** Here the multiple wires each hold two branches around a strong anchor (branch, wire, or trunk). Check there are no gaps between the branches and the wire, especially at branch junctions.

**Manipulate the branches to style your tree** and prune back further if necessary. Here, the apex will be pruned again at a later date, but all the stems are pointing in the right direction. In a few weeks the skeleton will fill out with new shoots.

# Making a broom-style bonsai

The upright trunk and rounded canopy of the broom style is almost exclusively associated with small-to-medium zelkovas and Chinese elms, but the techniques shown here are also useful for creating many other less formal shapes.

## Choosing suitable trees

The most suitable species for this highly stylised form are zelkovas and elms, but some maple cultivars are also used.

- **Look for a small-leaved tree** with a straight, scar-free trunk and even branching all the way round. A well-balanced *nebari* growing in all directions is a very desirable characteristic.
- **A small leaf type** is essential. The leaves of this zelkova are large, but it is easy to reduce their size.
- **Even branching** is important. Look for a small number of thicker branches with multiple thin secondary branches.

# Improve the branch structure

1 **Defoliate the tree.** This not only reveals the structure of the branches, but will also encourage a smaller leaf size. Remove the leaves one by one, snipping them off at the leaf stem. In most climates zelkova can be defoliated two or three times a year once the leaves have hardened off. Here, in midsummer, the leaves are hard to the touch, so can be removed. The following work can be done in winter as well as after defoliation in summer.

2 **Examine the structure** and identify any congested points or excessively strong growth. Nodes where multiple strong branches have been allowed to grow will soon thicken up and become unsightly. The secret to success is delicacy in the branches.

3 **Where there are two or more branches**, decide which ones to remove. It may be better to remove a thick branch and keep a thinner one as this not only improves taper but will often – as in this case – introduce a subtle change of direction. Straight lines indicate youthfulness whereas branch lines with movement indicate age.

4 **Use branch cutters** to take out thick shoot tips. Cut close and smooth to the trunk.

Overcrowded apex will benefit from pruning

You may be able to create a more delicate image by keeping thinner branches

# Prune the secondary branches

5

**Thin out dense or coarse shoots** in the remaining structure of primary, secondary, and tertiary branches. Aim to create a rounded overall shape with even branches all the way round.

Branch structure is even and well-balanced

6

**Assess the tree.** Look for areas that can be improved by wiring. Ideally it is best to use as little wire as possible, but here the apex and a few branches can be improved with repositioning.

7

**Wire the main branches** with a suitably thin gauge of aluminium wire. Avoid breaking delicate branches by wiring with your fingers, keeping your hands out of the tree and as still as possible.

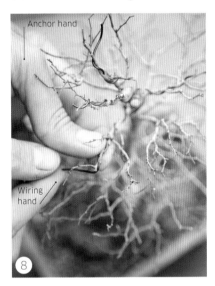

Anchor hand

Wiring hand

8

**Wire to the tip** but take care when the thickness of the wire is greater than the shoot. Here, the anchor hand holds the branch and wire secure while the wiring hand wraps the wire around the tip.

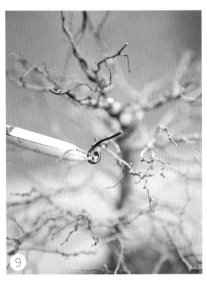

9

**Trim the ends of the wire.** Make sure you leave a wire tail that is long enough to prevent the branch jumping out of the wire and that allows you to manipulate the tip.

## Stop and relax

Wait for the best time to transplant – usually in spring, just as the buds start to swell. If this work is done in summer, prune back extensions on new growth to keep it in shape.

# Repotting your tree

Most upright deciduous trees look at their best in a shallow pot that creates an impression of growth in fertile lowland conditions. Repotting gives you the opportunity to choose a more attractive pot, correct the viewing angle, refresh the soil, and rejuvenate the roots. The need to repot varies according to the species, climate, soil, age, and development stage of the tree, but the basic technique is the same for all species.

**Check the correct front**. In styling this tree the front changed slightly from the original (*top*) to improve the relationship between the trunk and the branches.

# Prepare the new pot

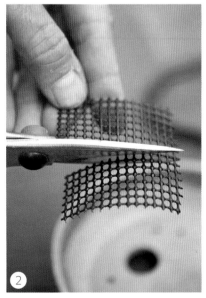

Bend the ends of the wire out to hold the mesh in place

**Cut a piece of plastic mesh** that will completely cover the drainage hole. This is to prevent soil from being washed away when watering.

**Bend a piece of wire into a U-shape.** Make the flat top section about the same size as the drainage hole so that the legs will fit tightly against the hole walls.

**Feed the staple** through the mesh and pull through. Bend the legs back until they are flat and smooth under the pot and the mesh is fixed securely in place.

# Remove the old soil

**Cut the wires holding the tree in the pot.** Always use at least two wires to secure the tree. If the tree is able to move in the pot, root development will be slowed.

**Use a root saw** to cut through the soil in contact with the pot walls. The aim is not to cut through any large roots, but to separate the rootball from the pot.

**Take the tree out of the pot.** Don't use force: if the tree is stuck, cut around a little more. With pines, try to avoid holding the flaky bark on the trunk.

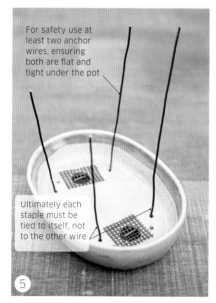

For safety use at least two anchor wires, ensuring both are flat and tight under the pot

Ultimately each staple must be tied to itself, not to the other wire

**Make anchor wires to secure the tree.** Use aluminium or stainless steel wire and a similar staple method, to feed the ends through the pot from the underside.

**Prepare the appropriate soil mix.** Sieve the soil to grade particle size and remove dust. Five minutes of effort can make a big difference to growth over two years!

**Cover the base with a layer of soil.** In deeper pots, a layer of larger particle soil is often used in the bottom of the pot to increase aeration in the soil.

**Gently rake out the soil** with a root claw. Always work radially from the centre outwards and never tear through roots; if you meet heavy resistance, then stop.

**Avoid damaging thick surface roots.** Your aim is to remove the soil and keep as many roots as possible.

**Use a bamboo chopstick** for finer areas and detailed work. Avoid sharp metal tools as they often damage the delicate roots. Always work radially outwards.

# Root prune and repot your tree

Remove any thick dominant roots

**Prune strong roots back hard.** For a well-balanced branching system, you need a well-balanced root system; do not allow any one root to become too strong.

**Trim fibrous roots down to size** with a sharp pair of root pruning scissors. Blunt scissors cause root development to slow down.

**Check the tree fits in the pot** in the correct position. Prune more roots if necessary, and add or remove soil as appropriate until the tree is well-seated.

**Cover the roots with soil.** Work soil in between the roots with a chopstick. Take care not to overdo it and push the roots to the surface or crush the soil to dust.

**Level the surface** leaving a very small lip at the pot edge; this will help to retain water. Do not over compact the soil.

**Water thoroughly** so that any dust and debris is washed out of the pot. This is a one-time opportunity to flush out dust: keep watering until the runoff is clear.

Avoid damaging surface roots with the wire

**17**

**Tie in the tree**. Use pliers to pull the wire over the roots, apply tension, then twist clockwise to shorten the wires. Repeat until the wires sit tight on the root base.

**21**

**Cover the surface** with a thin layer of shredded sphagnum moss to help retain water; remove the moss if you see roots develop into it in the next few months.

## The finished tree, after repotting

**Three months later** this zelkova has developed a new set of leaves. Prune back new growth, but do not defoliate immediately after transplanting a tree.

# Making a twin-trunk bonsai

Twin-trunk bonsai are inspired by multi-stemmed trees that occur naturally, perhaps when seeds germinate close together and merge to form one base. Use this simple technique to create your own twin- or triple-trunk designs.

## Choosing your material

Twin trunks are often described as parent–child combinations: the parent tree shelters the child as it grows up, out, and away.

- **Use cuttings from the same tree** to ensure identical features, such as leaf type and the timing of bud break.
- **Aim to choose** a straight, slightly larger, thicker, older-looking "parent" trunk, and a "child" that has a little more movement.

### The project aim

The straight trunk and branch structure make this the more obvious choice for the main tree

Subtle, natural movement will work well as the secondary trunk

# Prepare the roots

1 **Remove the pot**. This tree is only two or three years old and still in its plastic training pot, which has yet to fill up with roots.

2 **Carefully remove compost** with a root claw, working radially outwards from the trunk. The soil mix for young trees is usually loose and peaty, so falls away easily.

3 **Wash the roots** to remove the last of the soil mix if necessary. Avoid pressure-washing the roots, but use a hose-head jet feature if you need more power.

4 **Prune the strong tap root** back hard to favour the finer roots that surround it. Ultimately the trees will be planted in a shallow pot so it is a good idea to develop a healthy, fibrous root system from an early age.

# Position and plant the trees

5 **Plan your arrangement.**
Test the trees in various
positions and angles to find
the best fit in terms of trunk
movement, major branches,
and roots. Over time you
want the roots of the two
trees to fuse together to
create one large *nebari* from
which both trees grow. To
achieve this, make sure their
fine roots overlap, and do not
place the trees so far apart
that they remain separate.

6 **Choose the best design.**
Here the mother tree grows
straight up and the daughter
tree grows up and out at an
angle. Their roots will soon
mesh together to form one
big conjoined system.

7 **Position the mother tree**
to one side of the pot, leaving
slightly more room for the
daughter. Spread out the roots
to ensure they will grow in
all directions, particularly
those on the opposite side to
the second trunk.

8 **Cover with soil** and tamp
down a little to hold it in
place. Make sure you leave
enough space for the second
trunk. The soil mix includes
peaty compost ideal for low
maintenance and for root
development in young plants.

**Plant the daughter tree** as close to the mother as possible at the practised angle. Cover the roots with soil and tamp down gently to ensure the trees will not fall over.

**Leave the trees to grow on and develop roots**. If there is a spurt of rapid growth in the immediate future consider pruning back a little, but generally try not to disturb them other than basic pruning to shape, and the prompt removal of unnecessary major branches.

## Stop and relax

Trees need time to establish. Allow your tree to settle for at least half a growing season before moving on to the next stage.

# Shaping the secondary trunk

Anchor hand

Thumb holds last loop in place

This finger supports the branch and secures the earlier loop

Use one finger to guide wire into place for the next loop

12

Anchor hand

Wiring hand

13

Point defining the curve

14

11

**Wire the daughter tree.** Push the wire deep into the soil to ensure it is firmly anchored – there will be some roots in the pot now, and the soil should be compacted enough to give the wire something to push against.

12 **Wind the wire** up and along the trunk at a pitch of about 45° with your wiring hand. Use your anchor hand to support the trunk. Ensure the wire is not so tight that it damages the trunk, nor so loose that there are gaps between wire and trunk.

13 **Wire the trunk again** so that the second wire sits perfectly in the centre of the first set of coils. This will provide much more bending power without damaging the trunk.

**Bend the daughter trunk** to accentuate the space between the two trees. Slight and subtle movement is better than sharp changes of direction. Use your thumb to define the position of the bend, and support the trunk on either side.

**Finish off the styling.** Here some of the primary branches on the main trunk have also been wired to start them off in a more attractive direction.

# Creating a clump-style maple

The clump style is a scenic variation on the multi-trunk theme – typically five or seven trunks grow from one collective root base.

## Choosing your material

Clump styles are usually deciduous – maples, hornbeams, elms, and zelkovas are among the best. You want the trees to fuse into one *nebari*, so to ensure identical genetic traits, look for flexible young whips grown from cuttings taken from the same parent tree.

- **Think of a family** when planning your bonsai: a father and mother tree with three or five children reducing in size.
- **Look for** straight, thick parent trunks and subtle movement in the others.

### The project aim

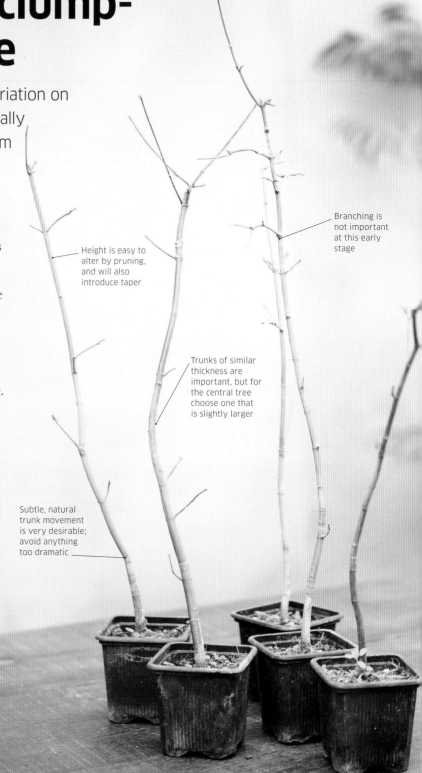

Height is easy to alter by pruning, and will also introduce taper

Branching is not important at this early stage

Trunks of similar thickness are important, but for the central tree choose one that is slightly larger

Subtle, natural trunk movement is very desirable; avoid anything too dramatic

# Preparing to plant

1 **Take the trees out of their pots** and carefully remove the soil. On young trees, like these two-year-old maples, soil should come away easily.

2 **Keep the bare-rooted trees in water** while you make the rest of the preparations. The trees will suffer if their roots are allowed to dry out.

3 **Prepare a training pot** for planting, securing mesh over any drainage holes, and inserting anchor wires (*see pp.130–131*). For this technique, one anchor wire will suffice. Part-fill the pot with a low-maintenance, water-retentive soil mix, including some compost.

4 **Prepare a piece of plastic.** Drill a series of holes, slightly larger than the trunks, in an asymmetrical arrangement to form an interesting clump.

**Take care** to consider the ultimate height and thickness of the clump you are making: the larger the trees of the final design, the greater the separation between them at planting. This example is for a *chuhin*-sized clump with relatively thin trunks.

Use a deep pot to establish the clump

Fix mesh with a wire staple

Strong, fairly rigid plastic sheet will sit in pot and hold trees in place

Anchor wire will be used to fix plastic

Holes are big enough to accommodate the trunks

# Creating the clump

5 **Thread the trees** through the holes: guide branches safely through, and take care not to damage any nodes. Place the straightest trunks in the middle and those with movement on the outside.

6 **Push the plastic** down the trunks as far you can without damaging the bark. It should stop just above the roots. Rotate trunks with movement to find the best combination and orientation, and set the clump on the soil surface.

7 **Make final adjustments** to the position and orientation of the trunks. Bring one anchor wire across the plastic then twist the ends together at one side, to ensure the plastic is held firmly in place.

8 **Cover the plastic** with a layer of soil, ensuring it is at least 1cm (¹/₄in) deep. This helps root development and compensates for the water-resistant barrier in the pot.

**Why so much soil?** Over time your trees will thicken up, and eventually outgrow the planting hole, causing tissue above the plastic to swell. As the plastic chokes the supply of nutrients from the roots, the trees send out new roots from the swollen area above the barrier – creating a new conjoined root system. The old roots will then be cut off, and the plastic removed.

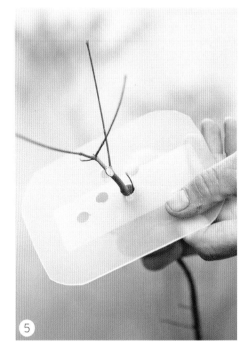

9 **Use a chopstick** to work soil down to the roots under the plastic barrier – but make sure you don't nudge the plastic or any of the trunks out of position.

10 **Water thoroughly.** If necessary set the pot at an angle to ensure that water gets to the roots underneath the plastic – and bear this in mind as you water the tree throughout the year.

11 **Chop up sphagnum moss** and spread a thick layer over the soil surface to retain moisture and encourage roots to develop above the plastic.

12 **Make some wire hooks** and use them to fine-tune the overall position of the shoots, pulling the trunks together or holding them apart as you require. Do not attempt to wire the trunks at this stage.

13 **Move the clump** to a sheltered spot, keep it well watered, and allow the tree to put on roots. The trunk position and movement should be set early in the development of the clump, so aim to make adjustments to the trunk positions in the first year by wiring once the roots are more established.

Wire loop helps trees to support each other

### Stop and relax

Allow the clump to establish before introducing any more movement – but make sure you do this in the first year. After two or three years the roots will be ready to separate.

# Creating a forest

Atmospheric forests are created by planting several individual trees together in the same pot. The tradition calls for odd numbers and for all the trees to be of the same species, but Japanese examples of multi-species forests do exist.

In forest plantings straight trunks are easier to deal with than those with strong movement

## Choosing your material

A huge range of coniferous and deciduous trees can be grown in the forest style. Popular choices include maple, stewartia, hornbeam, Hinoki cypress, pine, cedar, and larch – all of which naturally tend to grow in forests. Look for straight trunks of various sizes, and trees that have been root pruned at an early age to make them suitable for bonsai. There is no limit on the number of trees you can use, but displays of more than about 30 start to appear far too crowded.

- **Imagine the forest has self-sown**. Start with one main tree, then some slightly smaller and thinner trees, then double the number of even smaller and thinner "offspring".
- **Choose a tree with small leaves** and compact branching over one with coarse leaves and growth.

# Preparing to plant

1 **Prepare the trees.** Take each one out of its pot, carefully remove the soil, and prune off any strong roots (*see p.135*). Stand the bare roots in water until all the trees are ready (*see p.141*). Once all the trees have been prepared, lay them out in order of height and thickness.

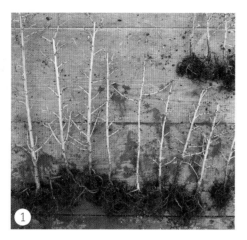

2 **Plan the basic structure.** The main trees will be tied down to a framework of bamboo chopsticks, so this is also an opportunity to figure out where they will be fixed.

Fix plastic mesh over the drainage holes (*see p.130*)

3 **Create the framework.** Lay out the chopsticks so that they intersect above the drainage holes.

Use a mica (plastic) training pot so that you can drill more drainage holes if you need them

4 **Position the frame.** Make sure that you can fix it firmly in place by threading wires through the drainage hole mesh. The central frame will secure the main trees and hold everything in place.

The central frame will be held in place with wires through four drainage holes

5 **Secure the framework,** wiring the ends together at intersections, and fixing it to the base of the pot using holes drilled for anchor wires. The chopstick frame should not move, but it must be possible for wire to pass underneath the chopsticks.

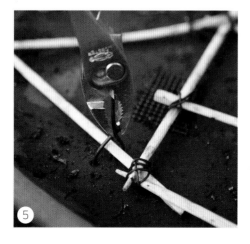

6 **Spread a thin layer of soil** across the whole pot. Use an appropriate soil mix for the chosen species (here, larch).

# Create the group

**Position the largest main tree**. Place it just off-centre, to one side and slightly towards the rear of the pot. Spread out the roots over the chopsticks, feeding thicker roots under the frame if possible.

Aluminium wires secure the tree to the frame

**Tie the tree in place**. Pass wire beneath the chopsticks and around the trunk so that it holds the tree securely. It is liable to move until soil is poured around it, – take care not to let it fall over.

**Take the next largest tree** and repeat the process. For a more natural effect arrange the trees so that there is more negative space in the foreground and to one side of the pot.

The main trunk is leaning at a dangerous angle so will need some support

**Stand back** and view the arrangement from all sides, checking the position and angle of the trunks. Make adjustments if necessary. It will be difficult to do this once the roots have grown together.

**Use keto soil** to change the position of the trunks if you need to. Build the soil up around the bases of the individual trees to nudge their trunks in a certain direction.

**Prune off branches** close to the base of each trunk to reflect the relatively bare lower trunks found in a natural forest habitat. Take care not to disturb the trunk positions.

Use a chopstick to work soil into the base of each tree

10

**Pour over soil** and slightly compact it on top of the roots of the planted trees as you work along. Once watered in, the soil will help to keep the tree in place until the roots develop sufficiently.

Reduce height to introduce taper, keeping the size in line with the rest of the trees

14

**Thin out branches** further up the trunk, especially those growing into the centre; keep one branch inside to every four or five outside to match forest conditions. Also consider the heights of each tree.

**Cover the tree roots with chopped sphagnum moss.** The freshly planted forest is extremely fragile. Move it to a sheltered place and leave it in the pot as long as you can to allow the tree roots to mesh together. Prune back strong growth, and remove strong surface roots.

# Creating a rock planting

Planting trees on rocks is a very enjoyable and creative process. To create believable miniature landscapes, all you need is an understanding of the long-term balance, a special type of clay soil, and a few extra tricks.

## Choosing your material

Most conifers and deciduous trees are suitable for rock plantings, but the character of the rock is more important. Wild and jagged rocks suit dramatic cascades or windswept styles; flat ones are good for forests or informal upright trees.

• **Bear in mind** that the rock will not increase in size, whereas the trees will.
• **The rock should not be so characterful** that it attracts too much attention.

**The finished display**

Flat area suitable for planting

*Shohin* size, and the drama in the trunk will work well as the secondary tree in a windswept pair

This windswept five-needle pine is a typical mountain species and matches the rugged image of the rock

This Ibigawa rock was worked and made suitable for bonsai, then imported from Japan

Rock sits securely in a stable position

# Prepare the rock

1 **Decide the orientation of the rock** and where the trees are going to sit. In this case a ready-made cavity will accommodate the trees with ease.

2 **Attach anchor wires to the rock** to hold the trees in position. Cut a long piece of copper wire, fold it in half to make a tight U-bend, and push the wire into a small crack. Bend the wire tails into an upright position and then pile a small amount of ready-mix concrete powder around the base, working it into the gaps.

3 **Carefully pour strong instant glue** onto the concrete powder; this should set hard within 5 seconds. Once hardened, add more concrete on top and repeat the process until the wire is firmly attached to the rock.

4 **Follow the same procedure** to attach at least two more sets of anchor wires. Use longer pieces of wire rather than too short. Put the rock to one side and allow to cure for at least ten minutes.

1

Ensure the copper wire is surrounded by concrete

2

Hold the wires in place until the glue sets

3

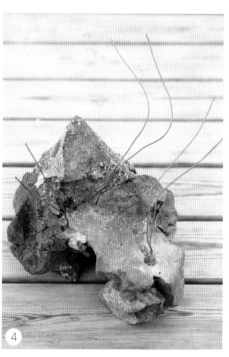

4

# Shape the trees and prepare the soil

5 **Aim to shape the trees** before they are placed on the rock to save moving them once they are in position.

6 **Thin out crowded areas** where more than three branches come from one point. The general rule is to avoid more than two branches from one node, but *shohin*-sized trees are the exception.

7 **Apply wire if necessary.** Avoid overworking the trees before planting: if they need lots of work, consider planting at a later date.

8 **The styled trees** can be fine-tuned later, but most of the work should be done before planting.

9 **Make up the clay mixture.** Chop up some sphagnum moss and mix it with keto soil, imported from Japan. Keto is a special type of very heavy, rich clay peat from submerged reed beds that hardens when dry. It is ideal for this job but similar local substitutes may be available.

10 **Firm the mixture into compact balls.** Make sure they do not crumble apart; if necessary add a little bit of water to make them more pliable. Balls of keto and moss store well, and can be kept for use at a later date.

Pruning the apex reduces the height and also restricts strong growth

5

Four branches from the same point is undesirable, even on *shohin* trees

6

Keep styling to a minimum to avoid stressing the trees just before planting

7

Tree is lightly shaped with just two or three pieces of wire

8

Moisture-retentive moss binds the clay together and increases structural integrity

9

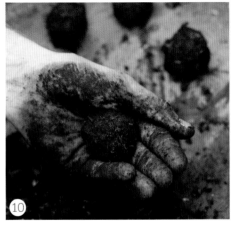

10

# Create the scene

**11 Prepare the first tree.**
Remove some – but not all –
of the old soil, and tease
out the roots (*see p.131*).

**12 Prune back large roots**
(*see p.132*). Aim to keep as
much of the fibrous root
system as possible, but test
the tree against the planting
space and trim back the
roots to ensure that it will
sit nicely in position on top
of a layer of soil mix.

**13 Make a keto "pot"**. Build
a wall of keto soil around the
edge of the rock, starting just
under the lip of the planting
shelf. Push it quite hard onto
the rock surface, and mould
it into shape; it should stay in
place easily. Once the wall is
in position, pour a layer of
small particle soil mix into
the planting area.

**14 Position the tree.**
Manipulate the roots to
reposition the trunk and
achieve the ideal orientation.

Check roots sit
comfortably in
the crevice

Press a ball of keto
against the rock and
mould it into a wall
to retain the soil

Keto pressed
firmly under the
planting shelf

# Finish the display

15 **Secure the tree,** bending anchor wires over the roots and twisting the ends together with pliers; be careful not to pull too tight in case the concrete fixing comes loose. Leave the tails long – they may be needed to fix the next tree in position.

16 **Put the second tree** in place, and tie in following the same procedure. Avoid moving the trees about to test how secure they are – you may inadvertently pull the wires out, concrete and all.

17 **Cover the roots with soil.** Use a bamboo chopstick to work soil in around the roots.

18 **Build up the keto wall** to contain the soil, moulding it piece by piece. The idea is to create a space for the tree to grow into, so do not make the planting pocket too snug.

19 **Leave the top open** for ease of watering and – in the absence of drainage holes – to aerate the soil if the keto becomes hard.

20 **Add a layer of moss** as a final touch, pressing three or four varieties onto the keto. Within a few months the moss should take root and start to grow, forming a natural framework that holds everything in place. Water thoroughly – but gently – to avoid washing everything off.

The open top allows oxygen to reach the roots if the keto becomes hard

Fix the moss in place by pushing small wire staples into the keto

**The finished tree**
• **Treat your rock planting** as a normal bonsai, but bear in mind it will be more susceptible to extreme conditions, such as temperatures over 30°C (86°F) or below 5°C (41°F).
• **Wait as long as you can to repot**. It does not need replanting as often as a tree in a pot; be guided by the soil surface and the vigour of the trees.

# Creating a *penjing*-style planting

Tray landscapes are one of the numerous styles and categories found in Chinese bonsai (*penjing*), and similar ideas exist in Vietnamese culture. They are often multi-species plantings on very Chinese-looking rock.

**The finished display**

## Choosing your material

Rocks for *penjing* styles are a little more jagged and stylized: they are often imported from China, where the distinctive shape is created by carving and bathing the rock in acid. Traditionally the Chinese use a special type of long, narrow oval *suiban* made from white marble to display the planting.

- **Remember** the rock will never grow any larger so consider the final desired size when planning the design.
- **Choose trees** for their movement and size. The Chinese elms and Japanese black pine here all offer a similar sense of scale.

# Preparing the trees

1 **Prune the branches** and shape each tree as if you were making it in a pot. Remove heavy branches to create an attractive structure. Once the trees are on the rock it will not be possible to do heavy work; in future they can be shaped by a clip-and-grow method (*see p.104*).

2 **Treat large wounds** on deciduous trees immediately with sealant. Try to ensure that any large wounds are on the back of the trees.

3 **Prepare the rootballs**. Take off the pots, and remove all the old soil from the roots of the deciduous trees (*see pp.130–131*). On conifers, tease out the roots and remove some – but not all – of the soil (*see p.151*).

4 **Untangle the tree roots**. Consider the planting position and angle at which each tree will be fixed to the rock, and look for roots that might get in the way or that could help to grasp the rock. Prune as necessary. Aim to compact the root ball as much as possible but do not prune so much that there are hardly any roots left.

Chinese elms can withstand heavy root pruning

# Planning and planting

5 **Check that the prepared trees fit** in their planting positions and make any final adjustments. Aim to wrap roots over or around the rock if possible. Look from the front and also the rear of the rock, considering where the soil and keto "pot" will go.

6 **Make planting cradles** out of plastic mesh to hold the trees in place if the rock has no natural crevices or flat surfaces. Keep the cradles as small as possible and slot them into any natural cracks and crevices.

7 **Attach copper fixing wires** to the rock with concrete and glue to keep the mesh in place (*see p.149*). Cut long pieces of thick wire strong enough to support the weight of soil and the tree itself – you can trim them down later.

8 **Place the mesh on top of the wires**, and cut the plastic to shape so that it fits snugly against the rock.

5

6

Fix the wires at points that cannot be seen from the front: this is the view from the rear

7

Cradle slots into a crack

8

Bend the wires up to surround the cradle

**9** **Mould the wires and mesh into a cradle.** Prepare a keto and moss mix (*see p.150*), and start to build a wall below the base to stop soil dropping through the mesh.

**10** **Position the tree.** Here the roots are firmly up against the rock and the tree has been squeezed into place. It is tight and secure without any anchor wires.

**11** **Gradually pour soil into the cradle.** Gently work the soil into and underneath the roots with a chopstick, taking care not to dislodge the tree.

Wires should curve up and over the top of the mesh

**12** **Carefully compact the cradle.** Apply just enough pressure to mould the cradle without disturbing it too much. Cover the outside with keto soil; if you have trouble making the keto stick to the mesh, add more sphagnum moss to the mixture.

A small gap in the keto at the base of the trunk allows oxygen and water to reach the roots

**13** **When the cradle is full,** trim off the ends of the wires and complete the keto wall until the tree is almost completely surrounded. If the keto looks dry or starts to crack, moisten your fingers with water and carefully smooth over the surface.

# Completing the scene

14 **Position the other trees using the same method.** If a tree cannot sit securely in a crevice, the wires can also be used to hold it in place. Thread the wires through the top end of the mesh, ensuring all the wires go through the mesh at similar points.

15 **Add soil to the cradle** then mould to shape, making it as small as possible. Wrap the wires around the trunk.

16 **Build a keto wall** around the cradle to help to keep the tree in place.

17 **Cover the keto with moss** fixing it with wire staples as necessary (see p.152). Take care not to disturb the cradle or the keto. They are initially very delicate but as the moss and trees start to grow, the arrangement will become much more secure.

**Water carefully** and position on the *suiban*. Consider the direction of the trees and the rock when positioning the display: leave more negative space in the direction of the flow of the composition.

• **Treat as a normal bonsai,** but bear in mind it is more susceptible to extremes, such as temperatures over 30°C (86°F) or below 5°C (41°F).
• **Wait as long as you can to replant.** Be guided by the soil surface and the vigour of the trees.

Thread wires through the mesh before adding soil

14

Wrap wires on both sides of the tree if necessary

15

For extra security cover the entire cradle with keto, right up to the base of the trunk

16

17

*"The overall image is of a rocky outcrop in the sea with much more of a landscape feel than a single tree...."*

# Making a root-over-rock bonsai

Inspired by trees clasped firmly to rocks in fertile forests and high mountainous areas, the root-over-rock style features tentacles of thick fleshy roots growing down over a rock and into the soil. This is a long-term project that takes years to develop, but creates extraordinary results.

## Choosing your material

Deciduous species such as Chinese elm (shown here), maples, and hornbeams are often seen as root-over-rock, but the style also suits most conifers. Look for young trees that withstand bare rooting: older ones may lose vigour. Start your tree off in a deep training pot, then transplant every other year, each time raising the tree a little further out of the soil and exposing more of the roots on the rock.

- **Choose a rock with definite movement** or an interesting feature, and aim to balance the character of the tree with the character of the rock.
- **The size of the rock will not change** so choose one that initially appears too large and out of balance with the tree – after about ten years they should start to match up.

Tree follows the same direction as the rock

Flat base will be under the soil and stable in the pot

# Prepare the pot

**You can use this technique** for any pot with only one drainage hole and no holes for wire.

1 **Cover the drainage hole with mesh** (*see p.130*). Cut a sturdy piece of chopstick slightly longer than the diameter of the hole to create an anchor point for the wires.

2 **Measure out anchor wires.** Check that the wire reaches the edge of the pot, allow a bit more, then bend the wire back on itself and match the length in the other direction. Repeat until you have four equal lengths in a W-shape.

3 **Cut the wire in half** to create two U-shaped wires with legs that are roughly the same length.

4 **Attach the anchor.** Wrap both wires around the chopstick, ensuring all the legs are the same length.

5 **Thread the wires through the mesh** from the underside of the pot, without disturbing the mesh. Check that the pot is stable and does not rock on the anchor point, and that the mesh will not be dislodged when the wires are tightened.

6 **Pour a shallow layer of soil** into the pot. Use a suitable soil for your tree. The soil used here is a normal bonsai mix including some compost – ideal for low-maintenance, rapid root development.

The anchor material should be relatively strong: a piece of thick wire or a headless nail make good alternatives

When measuring wire be generous with the length: you can trim it down later

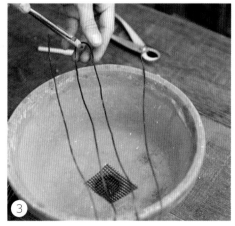

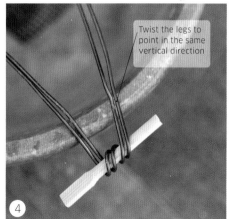
Twist the legs to point in the same vertical direction

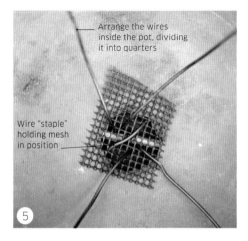
Arrange the wires inside the pot, dividing it into quarters

Wire "staple" holding mesh in position

# Prepare the tree

**Take the tree out of the pot.** Remove all the soil from the roots of deciduous trees (*see pp.130–131*). On coniferous trees, tease out the roots but aim to keep as much soil as possible (*see p.151*).

**Rinse the roots of deciduous trees** with water to remove residual soil if necessary. The thick, fleshy roots on this example are typical of Chinese elms, and ideal for training over a rock.

**Arrange fleshy roots over the rock.** If only fine roots are found, group together roots that start from similar positions on the trunk. Consider the best front of the tree and also of the rock.

# Plant and shape the tree

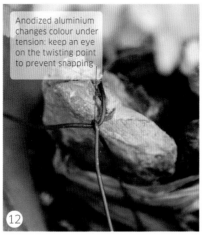

Anodized aluminium changes colour under tension: keep an eye on the twisting point to prevent snapping

**Position the tree and the rock** in the base of the training pot. On the first planting, the soil level must come right up to the base of the trunk, so make sure that you can plant deeply enough.

**Tie down the rock using the wires.** Work slowly, and take care not to pull the wires too tight: aluminium wire will snap easily if it is over-tightened or if it catches on a sharp edge.

**Cover the rock and tree roots with soil.** Bury as much of the rock as necessary to bring the soil level right up to the base of the trunk; this will encourage rapid root development. Lightly firm in.

**Bind the roots tightly to the rock** using pre-soaked raffia or organic twine. Apply considerable pressure: as the roots thicken they may try to grow out and away from the rock.

**Roughly style the tree.** With the orientation of the tree decided, you can now identify and remove unnecessary branches and thin out finer shoots. Apply wound sealant to the cut areas.

### Stop and relax

Style the top of the tree as normal. Transplant every other year, raising the rock each time. Aim to develop a fine root system below the rock, pruning back strong roots to prevent any becoming too dominant.

# Keshiki cotoneaster

Young trees planted in moss balls or modern containers have become popular amongst young, urban bonsai enthusiasts who live in apartments without a garden. They are a fun and inexpensive way to enjoy the seasonal beauty of bonsai, and are quick and easy to create.

Autumn fruits, evergreen foliage, and spring flowers offer plenty of seasonal interest

Tough, resilient cotoneaster is an easy, low maintenance species that may be grown indoors on a bright windowsill away from direct heat

Movement and fairly one-sided branching suggest a slanting style

## Choosing suitable trees

One of the most enjoyable aspects of bonsai is the seasonal changes it brings. Keshiki-type plantings are often used for fruiting and flowering deciduous trees that show this very easily, such as sumac, cotoneaster (shown here), azalea, or cherries. It is also possible with most conifers.

- **Consider the age and style of the tree.** Younger more elegant trees are best suited for keshiki, as are multiple seedlings grown in a tiny forest.
- **Be as creative as you want with pots:** there are no rules! Here, a cotoneaster is planted in a moss ball or *kokedama*.
- **Keshiki have a relatively short lifespan.** Be prepared to transplant after three or four years, and move them on to another keshiki-style planting – or even towards a more traditional bonsai.

# Prepare the tree

1 **Inspect the base,** removing any moss that is in the way. Always do this when styling a tree for the first time: a major problem or plus point with the roots will affect the design of the tree.

Remove branches from inside the trunk; shoots on the outside of curves are more pleasing to the eye

2 **Style the tree.** Remove lower branches, dead stumps, and unnecessary shoots. Stand back to consider the planting angle and position of the front. For a low-maintenance clip-and-grow approach, keep wiring to a minimum.

3 **Choose the front,** set the tree at the correct angle, and prune more of the branches to shape. Look to remove branches which are growing in undesirable directions.

4 **Continue to assess the tree** as you prune. Here, the aim is to leave as many berries on the cotoneaster as possible to be enjoyed when the styling is complete.

5 **Take the tree out of its pot** and start to reduce the root ball. Use a root claw to remove the soil and tease out the roots. Try to keep the root ball intact, working around it to create a spherical shape.

6 **Prune back the fine roots** with scissors to create a roughly spherical rootball.

# Create the *kokedama* ball

7 **Make up the keto soil mix,** combining it with sphagnum moss and work it into a ball (*see p.150*). Make sure it is structurally sound and does not crumble easily. Add more sphagnum moss if necessary.

8 **Create a planting bowl** by moulding the keto into the desired shape. Check the size of the hole against the rootball to ensure a good fit.

9 **Pour soil into the base.** Use a suitable small particle soil mix. Although the tree will be in there for several years the existing rootball will sustain it without the need for transplanting.

10 **Position the tree at the right angle** and fill the gaps with soil. There is no need to push soil in with a chopstick.

11 **Compact the keto ball** around the roots. Smooth off any cracks, and add more keto to the top if necessary. Mould the base a little to get the best angle for the tree.

12 **Cover the keto** with a carpet of mosses. Secure it with wire staples and black cotton thread; tie one end to an anchoring pin then wind it round and around the ball until it covers all the moss pieces. In about a month it will either be swallowed up by new mossy growth, or can be removed as the moss roots and holds the ball together.

Wire staples hold moss in place

**Caring for keshiki**

• **Water carefully for the first month**, and avoid using any high pressure water. Thereafter treat as a normal bonsai, but do not transplant until absolutely necessary.

• **Moss changes over the year**. Try to keep it moist in summer. It is perfectly normal for one variety to thrive while others die – moss is very particular as to where it will grow.

• **Display on your benches**, on a veranda, or for short periods of time in your home to appreciate a fun and playful side of bonsai.

# Rescuing a half-dead tree

Occasionally mistakes are made, pests or diseases strike, and bonsai suffers – sometimes half the tree even dies. But it is not necessarily the end of the line for your bonsai: with a bit of a rethink, trees like this hornbeam can have a great future.

Small leaves mean a smaller tree is possible

Dead trunk in centre

Trunk has only slight movement, so the original upright styling cannot change too much

Healthy shoots indicate strong roots and enough live vein activity to make a rescue worth pursuing

## What can you save?

Some trees will be past saving and should be planted in the ground or discarded. Species like azalea can be very difficult to resurrect once the live vein has been damaged. Look for trees with vigorous growth, which is evidence of healthy roots. Here, the long shoots on this Korean hornbeam indicate that its roots are strong and live veins are feeding the growth.

- **A drastic change of angle** can result in an interesting tree, so look from all different orientations and angles.
- **For inspiration** look at trees in nature that have been damaged and survived. A section of dead wood on the tree can make for an interesting character feature, especially on coniferous trees.

# Inspect, plan, and shape the branches

1 **Inspect the tree.** This hornbeam was previously at least twice the height, but has died back to a single branch, and exploded in a mass of leggy growth in all directions, concealing the half-dead trunk. Closer inspection shows three major branches coming from the same position, and a few smaller and weaker shoots emerging from the trunk. These tiny shoots are all trimmed off to leave the three major branches.

2 **Wire the major branches.** Manipulate them slightly to separate and spread out the growth: the aim is to create a definite branch structure. Once the main structure is in place, prune the secondary branches into shape. Remove or shorten any that grow back into the tree, directly upwards or downwards, and thin out areas that are too densely populated.

3 **Wire the secondary branches** after thinning, and bend them into position. These branches have not yet been pruned: it is much easier to manipulate long shoots.

4 **Prune the repositioned branches** into shape: imagine the outline of the foliage canopy, and make your cuts accordingly. Leave areas that need to grow slightly longer and prune back shoots that are already too long.

# Carving the dead wood

5 **Explore the dead wood.**
Remove any seriously rotten wood immediately. This may create very interesting character features – but it can also destroy them.

6 **Shape the hardwood,**
eating away at unnecessary sections bit by bit. Pay close attention to the ends of any *jin* – it should have slightly jagged edges – and also to the boundary between the live and dead sections. It is best to stop if you hit living tissue: the top layer under the bark will be a different colour, usually green or white, and it will be moist to the touch.

7 **The roughly carved dead wood feature** follows the established trunk line and has introduced a natural taper. When carving dead wood, aim to accentuate its natural character, such as knots or exposed grain.

8 **Smooth off rough edges.**
Use a rotary tool with a carving or sanding bit to remove very small amounts of wood, bring out the grain, and remove any obvious tool marks. Power tools can be used to remove and style large amounts of dead wood, but do take care not to make it look too artificial.

**The finished tree** now has a basic structure defining the branches and what was once a dead and unsightly feature has become a character point.

Remove bark from the dead section with spherical knob cutters, along with soft, rotten wood

5

6

7

8

# Making a juniper cascade

If you manage their foliage with care and understanding, versatile junipers perform in any number of styles – including dynamic cascades.

## Choosing suitable trees

Look for material with plenty of mature foliage that will make a tree with minimal amounts of branch removal. The foliage is very important; this is 'Itoigawa', a popular cultivar with compact growth, small leaves and a vibrant green colour.

- **Always consider adjusting the planting angle**. Think ahead before you style the tree: the angle can be changed next time you transplant.
- **Two strong branch lines** and a strong *nebari* are ideal for a good cascade.

**The finished cascade**

Vibrant green juvenile foliage has been cut back hard in the past

This combination of one strong branch with a shorter more upright trunk will make an ideal cascade, especially when the planting angle is adjusted

# Create the overall shape

1 **Examine the tree** from all angles and orientations, then choose the one that offers the best balance between the trunk and branch lines, as well as holding the *nebari* on the side opposite the cascade. You can set a temporary new planting angle by balancing your tree on an empty training pot.

2 **Assess the tree at its new angle.** Aim to remove any branches that appear to be growing against the flow of the cascade, and gradually thin out the structure. Here, the secondary shoots from a small branch are removed one by one.

3 **Constantly stand back** to check your work. In this case, with all the secondary shoots removed the small stump that remains is perfectly placed to create a new dead wood feature.

4 **Continue to thin out the structure.** Here, a few more branches have been removed from the cascading branch, and you can clearly see the line of the branch and trunk. The initial idea was to reduce the upward-growing trunk that forms the apex – however this is impossible to do without cutting back to a very thin branch, and may have an adverse affect on the health of the tree.

Stump will be stripped back to make a *jin* or *shari*

# Thin out and clean juniper foliage

Cleaning the foliage is a very delicate task: your tree will suffer if you "pinch off" growing tips in this rough manner

5

Dark green non-growing foliage is often internal but may also be a leaf that flowered the previous year

Active growing tip

6

7

**Carefully clean the foliage** when the structure is set. The light green growing tips at the end of the foliage are essential for the health of your tree (*see p.117*).

**Look at each tiny leaf** and identify the ones without active growing tips. It should be easy to tell the difference – active tips are a vibrant light green.

**Remove all inactive growth**. This will stimulate fresh new growth with active tips; if necessary the branch can be compacted to create a denser foliage pad.

# Wire the cascading branches

Use a suitable gauge of copper wire

11

12

13

**Wire the tree**. On this example the main trunk has a pleasing shape and does not need to be manipulated. Only the main secondary branches need to be shaped.

**Always wire branches in pairs** so that they can support each other. Remember to support the branch with one hand while wiring with the other (*see p.138*).

**Apply the wire** at a slightly stretched out pitch: a 55° angle is ideal, as seen here from below. This allows branches to be lowered and separated a little.

**Prune long vigorous extensions** back into shape. Removing the tips will cause the sideshoots to develop further, encouraging a dense foliage pad.

**Look for junctions** with two strong, viable secondary shoots – both with active growing tips – then prune back the tip to leave the two sideshoots.

**Plenty of active growing areas** remain on the pruned shoot. They will continue growing and will need pruning again in the same way as the sideshoots develop.

**Manipulate the branches** after all of the main structural wires have been applied. Here, one or two bends in the branch will make a big difference to the tree.

**Always apply pressure carefully** and make sure there is wire on the spine of the bend. Here, the branch is bent down and towards the front.

Upper trunk area has yet to be shaped

Outline of the foliage now cascades down

**Follow the direction of the tree**. Here the re-shaped branch continues the flow of the cascade; the lower pad has a wider spread – both left to right and vertically.

# Shape the top of the tree

**17 Consider using guy wires** to shape the upper trunk. Here the trunk needs to be compacted back towards the right-hand side, and guy wires are a less intrusive alternative to heavy wire. Identify a point on the main trunk where the guy wire can be attached that will not tear away when pulled. Thread a length of copper wire through a rubber hose and ensure the wire tails are the same length.

**18 Select a fixing point at the base**. This is where the two ends will be tightened. Never tighten the guy wire halfway along, always at one end or the other.

**19 Hold the hose in place** and use pliers to pull the wires tight. Stop pulling when tension has been achieved then twist clockwise until taut. When using a guy wire, always use one hand to move the branch – or ask for a second pair of hands – and tighten with the other, so that when pulling the wire taut, you do not move the branch as well. Here, while the pliers hand pulls to achieve tension, the other hand bends the trunk towards the base.

**20 When the branch is in position**, use a piece of chopstick and twist the guy lines together to hold the branch in place. Do not over-tighten as the wires may snap.

Hose protects the tree from damage when wire is pulled tight

Twist once to secure the wire but do not choke the trunk

17

Slit one side of the second hose to allow access to both ends of the wire

18

19

20

**The finished tree** will be planted at the new angle when it is next transplanted; ideally keep it at the correct angle until then. The foliage pads will be allowed to grow while juvenile and leggy foliage is removed and adventitious buds develop.

# Twisted dead wood juniper

Powerful dead wood features are a great character point of coniferous trees. To recreate the effect in a container, look for examples of trees in nature or masterpiece bonsai.

## Choosing suitable trees

Dead wood features occur on most conifers but each is defined by the natural growth habit. Get to know the live vein characteristic of the species – specifically how directly a live vein connects a root to a branch – junipers are very linear, but pines are more dynamic. The techniques are the same, but their application differs.

- **Look for trees with twisted trunks** where the live vein rotates around.
- **Choose material** with lots of unnecessary branches that can be removed leaving stumps for *jin* or *shari*.

Several long branches will be easy to manipulate

Strong surface root is likely to be the main root for the entire tree

Twist in the trunk where the live veins rotate around it is ideal for creating a dead wood feature

**Restyled and carved tree**

# Creating dead wood from living tissue

1 **Try to trace the strong live veins** to identify areas you can remove without affecting the branches. Look for raised areas or strong lines working from the branches down, or from the roots up. Here, the chopsticks show two major points – a twist in the trunk with a depressed area of live vein, and a major root. Live veins are like muscles: the more they are used the bigger they get, so you can assume the strong root carries a large amount of nutrients, and the depressed area does not.

2 **Mark the area to remove** with chalk or a marker pen. Start with a fairly thin line and flow with the grain, not across it. Avoid areas directly below branches and do not cross strong veins. Follow the bottom of the valley but also check that the line of dead wood is attractive: ideally avoid making straight lines.

3 **Cut the edges** either side of the line with a sharp chisel, pushing through the soft top layer until you hit hard wood. Once you have defined the area to lift, prise up the entire section of live material.

4 **Use pliers** or your fingers to pull gently in the direction of the fibres. If the grain takes you in an undesirable direction, stop and reconsider where it is going. Cut off the end of the live vein. If you are confident the main veins will not be damaged, then chisel it out again.

Strong root will supply a large amount of the tree's nutrients

Depressed area is less important to the tree: fewer nutrients travel through it

1

Dead wood features on junipers spiral irregularly around the trunk as if they have been caused by severe conditions

2

Edges of the marked area are defined for about two chisel widths, following the grain of the tree

3

4

Pull back the entire section of bark and cambium layer

# Clean and polish the trunk

5 **Gently clean the bark if necessary.** Juniper bark can be very flaky: on some species this adds character, but for others it appears dirty. Here, removing it refines the image and also adds contrast to the reddish live vein and the white dead wood. Take care not to scrub so hard that you expose the pink-purple live vein. Stop if you see this.

6 **Tidy the *shari*,** but do not do much detailed work. The freshly made dead wood is full of moisture and must dry out before it is refined. Never apply lime sulphur to brand new *shari* or *jin:* it will kill off the cells if it gets into the live vein through the wounds.

Remove flaky bark with a wire brush

Smooth off fibres on the *shari* with a wire brush or sander tip on a rotary tool

# Shape the tree

7 **Assess your tree** and fine-tune your plan now that the dead wood has been created. Remove unwanted branches, leaving stumps for a *jin* or to continue the *shari*. Remember not to remove more than 40 per cent of the foliage in one go (*see p.117*).

8 **Wire the tree** and set the main structure. Apply fine wire to secondary shoots, but keep in mind the amount of live vein removed from the tree: too much work on the branches could cause the tree to stall and then stagnate. Leave active growing tips at the ends of the branches to ensure the tree continues to grow without skipping a beat.

**The finished tree** will be planted at a new angle at the next transplanting. The live vein is now clearly visible flowing up from the strong root at the base, twisting around the trunk, into the main branch, and splitting off into the upper shoots and apex. It is not always easy to read live veins, but with careful observation of the tree you can find the correct path.

# Refining a windswept pine

Sometimes subtle changes to a styled tree can result in a much-improved bonsai. Commercial growers in Japan and China are adept at creating semi-styled material that is waiting for someone to put their mark on it; even small changes can take a tree to a much higher level.

**The finished tree**

## Choosing suitable trees

Commercially grown material often follows a pattern, so a nursery may have several similar semi-styled trees.

- **Look for obvious possibilities.** This imported Zuisho white pine has dynamic movement in its slanting trunk, with branches growing to one side – a windswept style, perhaps?
- **Look for characterful features.** On this tree the lower branch is very interesting, sweeping below the dense canopy.
- **Consider the habit.** Here the compact growth, ability to back bud, and the small needle size are ideal for a small-to-medium tree.

# Assess the angle and structure

**Inspect the *nebari* at the base.** Use tweezers to clean away soil and moss to expose any character points – both good and bad. Here, the sphagnum moss has been hiding some interesting dead wood.

Area of pale dead wood

**To explore the extent of dead wood** carefully remove the bark until you hit living tissue – on pines the difference is easy to spot. Stop when you get to the edge, and clean up the exposed wood.

**Assess the front view.** This pine has one strong root and an interesting dead wood section in the base; the tree can be angled so that both will be seen from the front, with branching towards the right.

# Create new features

**Identify unsightly branches.** Here, two branches growing upwards go against the flow of the tree. They were left to help thicken up the trunk, but can be used to make a dead wood feature (*jin*).

A long stump can be reduced in stages to create a more natural effect

**Create new dead wood.** Pines have soft, fast-growing wood that rots quickly, so stumpy *jin*, exposed *shari*, and hollowed out trunks often occur naturally. Cut off the branch, leaving a long stump.

The newly created *jin*

**Refine the stump and create the *jin*.** Strip the bark by crushing and pulling it away with pliers, or tear off the layers with branch pruners to expose the grain, creating a rough, torn appearance.

# Thin out buds and branches

Three buds are selected: two grow horizontally, and the third is growing upwards at a 45° angle

**7**

**8**

Roughly pruned branches help to define the structure and set the front angle before manipulation

A short piece of wire marks the new front viewing angle

**9**

**Thin congested buds.** 'Zuisho' white pine produce up to eight buds from one node. Reduce to two or three shoots of similar size growing in the right direction.

**Prune back strong, bare, leggy shoots.** New growth will develop faster from internal buds, allowing you to build up secondary and tertiary branches.

**Mark the front.** If necessary, correct the angle next time the tree is transplanted. When this tree is repotted, the new front will be squared up to the edge of the pot.

# Wire and shape the tree

Thick wires allow the character branch to be lowered and brought towards the front

**10**

Wire on the spine of the branch helps to prevent snapping and will hold it in place afterwards

**11**

**12**

**Wire branches that need to be moved,** setting the main structure with heavier gauge wires. Aim to create a sound, attractive, and sustainable framework.

**Always bend branches with two hands.** Use your fingers and thumbs to define the curves, as well as to support the branch and prevent it snapping.

**Make multiple bends** along the same branch to ensure secondary shoots are pointing in ideal directions. This will reduce the need for lots of fine wiring.

**The finished tree**
• **Next spring** the tree will be transplanted into a more attractive pot, correcting the front angle.
• **Over the next three years** with careful pruning, bud selection, and corrective wiring the branches will fill out and become more refined.

# Making two trees from one

Air layering is a superb technique that allows you to create new bonsai almost instantly from the branch of a garden tree, or the apex of overgrown bonsai. It is relatively easy to do, and deserves a place in the armoury of every bonsai enthusiast.

**The finished trees, four months after layering**

## Choosing suitable trees

Most trees can be layered, but for best results choose relatively young and vigorous deciduous trees; conifers are generally more difficult.

- **Look for interesting branches** or upper sections of trunk that would make a great tree if it only started further up.
- **Layer the apex of a bonsai** to create an almost finished *shohin*.

After a couple of years of rough pruning and shaping the top section has a good, well-ramified structure

The long, slender trunk has very little movement and no lower branches

A long, vigorous lower branch that could become the new leader of a much shorter tree

**This Japanese maple** is too thin for a large tree, and branches at the top are thick compared to those lower down. Dividing it into two will make the most of the structure at the top, while a second smaller tree can start life with an ideally placed new leader.

# Prepare the tree for layering

**Decide the position and angle of the layer.** Normally it will be horizontal but it is possible to create an angled layer. Remove any branches that are going to be in the way.

**Check the diameter of the trunk** and calculate the size of the layer. For best results it should be approximately one-and-a-half times the diameter of the trunk or branch.

**Measure the distance from the top downwards** and make a small mark so you know roughly where to make the cuts. You do not have to be accurate to the last millimetre: this is just a guide.

**Use a clean sharp knife** and make the upper incision: cut through the cambium layers to the heartwood in a straight line all the way around the trunk. Do exactly the same at the bottom of the layer.

**Carefully score a line down the trunk** to join the two incisions together, making sure that you cut right through to the heartwood.

**If necessary slide a chisel under the skin** and use it to help prise the collar of cambium tissues away from the heartwood.

# Treat the wounded area

Top cut is sharply defined

**(7)**

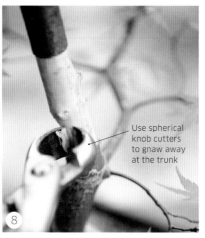

Use spherical knob cutters to gnaw away at the trunk

**(8)**

**(9)**

**Peel off the skin**. Remove any sections that remain and then tidy up the top cut, making sure that the top line is clean and well defined.

**Remove a small section of heartwood** – not so much that it will affect the structural integrity of the trunk, but enough to damage the surface and prevent the wound forming a callus.

**Apply root hormone in liberal amounts** to the upper cut: use gel, or make a paste of powder with a tiny amount of water to ensure it is not washed or brushed off over the next few steps.

# Two months later: reveal the roots

**(13)**

**(14)**

**(15)**

**When you can see that plenty of new roots** have formed throughout the layer, and the package feels slightly compacted to the touch, it is time to remove the plastic.

**Carefully unwrap the plastic** and look to see whether delicate new roots have formed all around the trunk. They are extremely fragile, so take great care as you separate the two trees.

**Remove the top section.** Cut through the trunk with a saw, but be very careful not to damage either the roots, the lower branch, or your hand.

**Cut a transparent plastic sheet** large enough to wrap around the trunk and fix it at the bottom either with a stapler or by wrapping wire around the trunk. Check the base is fairly tight and secure.

**Pack the layered area with moistened sphagnum moss**, and wrap the plastic around it, compacting as you go. Do not place too much moss above the upper wound: stop about 2.5cm (1in) above it.

Keep the layer and soil in the pot well watered

Rotate 90° each week to ensure each side gets enough sun

**Secure the plastic with wire** and keep everything from moving. Do not over compact or close off the top too much: try to make a slightly open funnel at the top with space for water to be added.

The new leading shoot

**Now you have two trees!** Here the top section has developed an entire root system of its own, and the bottom tree now has a new leader – what was once the lowest branch of the original tree.

Use tweezers to remove as much moss as possible

**Remove as much moss as you can**. If necessary gently dunk the layer in a bucket of water to help loosen it. A little moss will not harm the tree but large amounts may cause root rot in future.

**Saw off the old trunk to make a neat radial root system**. Ease back the roots, tip the tree up, and cut the trunk back to within a few centimetres of the new roots to create a very flat-bottomed tree.

# Finish the two trees

**Prepare a training pot**, and pour small particle soil mixture around the roots. The roots are easily damaged, so do not work the soil into them too much.

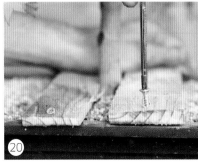

**The tree must be kept still to establish**, but the roots are too delicate for fixing wires to be effective. Here a wooden brace is made to hold the tree in place.

**Water well**. When the water runs clear, cover the soil with chopped sphagnum moss to retain moisture, and carefully move to a sheltered position.

**Do not forget the base of your original tree.** Trim the area below the separation and make a plan for the new base of the trunk.

**Tidy the wound** until the line flows smoothly from the trunk into the new leader. Take care to get the right line even if it means making a larger wound.

**Apply wound sealant** then leave it alone until next year: the more foliage it has, the better the wound will heal. Do not prune until after the leaves have fallen.

**Two months after their separation** both trees are thriving, and ready to drop their leaves in autumn.

• **The layered tree** Avoid moving or disturbing it until the following summer to give the roots time to develop, but provide winter protection: it is essential the roots never freeze.

• **The lower trunk tree** For the next year the focus will be on healing the wound caused by the air layering, and thickening up the trunk by pruning after leaf fall.

# Bonsai from the very beginning

It takes many years of patient care and the correct cultivation to create a masterpiece bonsai – but it helps if the tree is set in the right direction from year one. In many ways the first few steps are the most important: this is how to start the journey on the right foot.

**The repotted seedling**

These Japanese black pines were sown in spring and are now approximately six months old

## Raising trees from seed

Bonsai seeds are exactly the same as those that create normal trees: there is nothing special about them. What is special is the way in which seedlings are treated after germination.

- **The seeds of each species** require different processes of stratification, sowing, and soil to thrive, so refer to the instructions supplied, or buy seedlings from a bonsai nursery.
- **To create a compact tree** with lots of compact branches, you also need a compact and well-ramified root system. To achieve this, prune the roots of your seedlings during the first year after germination.
- **Do not put all your eggs in one basket:** sow and plant up 100 seeds. After a few years, give half of them away to friends, and wire the remaining trees. After a more few years, reduce these to the best ten, and so on – until you are left with one incredible tree and you have spread the joy of bonsai to another 99 people.

# Lift the seedling and prune the roots

1 **Carefully lift a strong seedling** from the tray. Most trees send out a long tap root, which is designed to burrow into the earth to give the tree stability; once this has been achieved, fibrous lateral roots develop. For bonsai you only want to encourage the fine, lateral roots – and by pruning back the taproot even more of these finer roots will form.

2 **Spread out the roots** on a clean, hard surface. Identify the taproot, and decide where you can safely cut it back. In very warm climates, such as Japan, black pine seedlings like these may have all their roots removed; they are then treated as fresh softwood cuttings, which leads to a completely fibrous root system. In cooler, more temperate climates in which black pines grow more slowly it is better to be cautious and retain some of the roots.

3 **Cut through the tap root** using a very sharp, clean knife. The cleaner the cut, the better the chance of root development.

4 **The root-pruned seedling** is left with lateral roots only – and the makings of a fine fibrous root system.

In just six months the seedling has developed a very long taproot

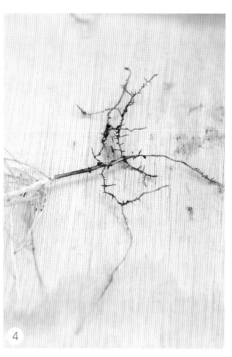

## Pot up the seedling

**Prepare a small training pot.** Smaller is better in this case because it will warm the roots more rapidly. Insert a piece of drainage mesh and cover with a layer of large particle soil to increase aeration.

**Plant the seedling** in a very fine particle soil mix – here pumice, akadama, and kiryu. You can use the fines from sieving out large particle sizes; make sure it is tiny particles (not dust) and use plenty of very fine lava or pumice which improve the soil structure, increase aeration, and will not break down.

### Stop and relax

Put the seedlings in a sheltered place initially; move them into the sun once they have started to grow. Consider the tree you want to develop: a tall literati requires different treatment to a *shohin* cascade. If appropriate, prune back woody terminal growth; this encourages new buds to form lower down the trunk that can eventually become the lower branches.

## Shaping young whips

The next stage of development is the first wiring, when the trunk shape and style is set. Try to think ahead, be adventurous, and don't be afraid to put dramatic movement into the trunk at this early stage. Here the do's and don'ts of wiring can be seen on two Scots pines as the straight whips begin their transformation into literati trees.

Strong terminal growth with several branches is left for now

Long, branchless trunk may develop new buds if the top growth is pruned back hard

For a literati tree, leave these little shoots to develop some extra girth in the lower trunk

The first node: in future the strong top growth will be pruned back to this point leaving two small shoots, and causing new buds to form

To create a *shohin* tree, cut the main trunk right back and use one of these branches as the new leader; there will be an explosion of new growth

# Starting a literati design

**Double wire the trunks** with thick aluminium wire, pushing it deep into the soil to secure the base. Avoid using re-straightened wire that has been removed from previously wired trees.

**Wire the full length of the trunk.** You can also arrange the second wire so that it sits between the first (see p.138). The wires will be removed in a few months: there is no need to make it look pretty.

**To add dramatic movement,** start at the base of the trunk and work your way up, bending to left and right, and from front to back. The trunk is very flexible and can be bent almost at right angles.

**Use both hands,** and ensure the wire is on the outside of the bend. Aim to create almost random movement, varying the intervals between each bend, so it looks attractive and natural.

**Fluid motion has transformed one tree into a visual treat;** the other remains somewhat dull and two-dimensional. Leave the wire in place until it just starts to dig in, then remove immediately. You may need to rewire the trunk, but try to keep the same shape, and do not attempt to restyle.

# Wild collected trees

Working with *yamadori* is an exciting challenge for the bonsai artist. It can be difficult – but very rewarding – to combine the natural character with your own ideas. Material can be expensive, but trees like this pine provide enthusiasts with an excellent introduction to *yamadori* trees.

## The finished tree

Slightly leggy branches with strong buds and foliage indicates great vigour

## Choosing suitable trees

Trees are generally left in the pot for several years after collection to allow them to establish and gain some vigour; not all are easily made into a bonsai. Roots, branches, and unique character are the three main points to consider.

- Choose a tree with an established rootball – you can't be sure it is trouble-free until you transplant, but avoid any obvious problems.
- Look for branches close to the trunk: it can take years to develop adventitious branches.

Trunk with subtle movement and aged bark

Tree is well established with plenty of roots and no obvious problems – avoid any with dominant roots extending out from the tree that would need heavy manipulation to fit in a suitable pot

# Thin out the framework

**Thin out major nodes**. On this example, three branches are growing from one spot, so the thin, leggy branch growing out to what will become the front is removed to leave two major branches.

**Leave a long stump** to give yourself the option of creating a *jin*. Using pliers, carefully crush the branch just a little so that the living tissue separates from the heartwood, and can be easily removed.

**Create the *jin*.** Pull back the bark, tearing it along the natural grain until it reaches the desired point. Do not go too far on the trunk. Roughly style the end of the *jin* so that it looks more natural.

**Remove other unnecessary branches** from crowded nodes then step back to choose the front, planting angle, and plan. Think ahead before pruning and wiring and you will create a better tree.

**This tree grows at an angle**, but the idea here is to make it a little more vertical. The change of angle will bring the apex over the base of the trunk creating the foundation of a well-balanced literati-style tree – very much in keeping with the natural growth habit of Scots pine.

# Shaping the branches

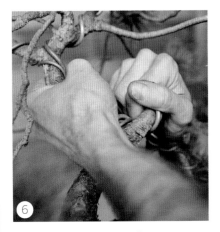

**Apply heavy structural wire** to the main branches, depending on how much they need to be bent, according to your plan. Pines are very flexible – even old, thick branches can be bent with double wires.

**When manipulating branches**, always use both hands to make severe bends, and consider – and support – weak spots such as branch junctions and dead wood features where damage may occur.

**Use guy wires** to help bend and hold heavy branches. Here, the branch is bent with slow, controlled pressure, while the pliers twist the guy wires taut around a *jin* without pulling the branch down.

**Stand back and assess the tree.** With the main branches in position, it is time to decide what you want to do with the secondary branches, and plan your pruning and wiring accordingly.

**Remove unnecessary branches**, where another branch can do the same job. Try to compact longer branches, cutting back where possible. Remember that branches can be lowered to fill in space.

**Wire secondary and tertiary branches** after pruning. In this case almost every branch was wired. Thin out tertiary branches and old foliage as you wire, in order to achieve a cleaner image.

The guy line is threaded through the structural wire

Guy line is anchored around a *jin*

**9**

**Twist the guy lines together**
using a waste piece of heavy wire
to tension it. Stop twisting as
soon as you achieve full tension
– otherwise the wire may snap.

**13**

**Wire the whole tree before you style it.**
It is always a good idea to complete the
wiring before you do any fine work to
avoid damaging styled lower branches
as you work your way up the tree.

**On this styled tree** the foliage has been arranged into
neat, well-organised pads; movement in the branches
has added interest and compacted leggy branches.
After a few years of careful pruning and foliage
management it will appear a lot more natural.

# Plant care directory

This directory provides a brief description and summary of care for many of the most popular trees and shrubs used for bonsai, listed in alphabetical order by botanical name.

## Key to hardiness

Plant entries have been given hardiness descriptions and zone numbers as follows:

**Frost tender** Plant may be damaged by temperatures below 5°C (41°F).
**Half hardy** Plant can withstand temperatures down to 0°C (32°F).
**Frost hardy** Plant can withstand temperatures down to -5°C (23°F).
**Fully hardy** Plant can withstand temperatures down to -15°C (5°F).

**Hardiness zones** developed by the United States Department of Agriculture are often used as indicators of plant hardiness. They are based on average annual minimum temperatures in given geographical areas (see http://planthardiness.ars.usda.gov/PHZMWeb/). The zone rating for each plant indicates the coldest zones in which it can survive winter. Bear in mind that other factors including altitude, exposure to wind, and the intensity of cold also affect hardiness – and that bonsai may be more vulnerable for being in a pot, so take the time to get to know conditions in your own garden.

**Zone 1** below -46°C (-50°F)
**Zone 2** -46 to -40°C (-50 to -40°F)
**Zone 3** -40 to -34°C (-40 to -30°F)
**Zone 4** -34 to -29°C (-30 to -20°F)
**Zone 5** -29 to -23°C (-20 to -10°F)
**Zone 6** -23 to -18°C (-10 to 0°F)
**Zone 7** -18 to -12°C (0 to 10°F)
**Zone 8** -12 to -7°C (10 to 20°F)
**Zone 9** -7 to -1°C (20 to 30°F)
**Zone 10** -1 to 4°C (30 to 40°F)
**Zone 11** 4 to 10°C (40 to 50°F)
**Zone 12** 10 to 15°C (50 to 60°F)
**Zone 13** 15 to 21°C (60 to 70°F)

## Abies
### FIR

True fir trees are not often used because they are generally unsuitable for bonsai techniques. A number of dwarf varieties that are more suited to *shohin* trees can be found in garden centres, but classical styling may be difficult. Species include *A. alba* (silver fir), North American native *A. grandis* (grand fir), Korean fir *A. koreana* and its cultivar 'Compact Dwarf', as well as *A. lasiocarpa* (alpine fir), which is perhaps the most suitable species for cultivation in a container.

All are hardy (zones 3–7); these mountainous conifers tolerate cold, but it is essential to protect the pot and roots in extreme freezing conditions. Protect from cold, drying winds and provide shade in intense summer sunlight. They prefer well-drained soil as they suffer from root rot. Treat in a similar way to spruce (*Picea abies*).

## Acer
### MAPLE

There are numerous varieties of this deciduous tree, and many are classic species for bonsai. Grown for their year-round appeal, maples look refined and elegant in winter with their naked branches; vigorous in spring with delicate new shoots; cooling in summer with a luscious canopy of foliage; and they come into their element in autumn as the leaves turn vibrant shades of red, yellow, and orange.

Each of the popular bonsai varieties have their own idiosyncrasies – initially it is best to stick to these varieties, as their growth habit is more suited to bonsai cultivation. Many cultivars are selected for a specific growth habit, such as weeping or cascading – do not try to go against that. When using cultivars not named here, look for small leaf and node size in order to create a compact bonsai shape. Maples can be defoliated to increase ramification and reduce leaf size, but this depends on the vigour of the species as well as the individual tree, the time of year, and growing conditions.

**Hardiness/Position** Some varieties are more frost tolerant than others; in general maples are frost hardy (zones 5–8) but should be protected from any deep freezing of the roots. If temperatures regularly drop below freezing for extended periods, winter protection is essential. When new shoots are breaking in spring or after defoliation in summer, provide protection from intense sun and wind. Otherwise they are happy in full sun, but appreciate semi shade in intense midday sunlight during the height of summer.

**Watering** Maples can be very thirsty species in the spring/summer period when new buds are opening and when in full leaf: it is very important not to allow the leaves to dry out at this time through lack of moisture. During winter in cold climates with average temperatures of 5°C (41°F) the soil may remain moist from November until March; do not overwater for fear of causing root damage through freezing. In warmer climates the roots are still active, so monitor soil moisture levels.

**Fertilizing** Use a well-balanced organic fertilizer – but the rate and timing of application depends on the tree and its stage of development. If the tree is still in the early stages and thickness and rapid growth is required, fertilize heavily from bud break in spring until leaf drop in autumn, with a break in midsummer when average temperatures rise to 32°C (90°F) and over. For more developed trees where the goal is delicate ramification, only fertilize lightly once the buds have opened, been pinched, and the leaves have opened and hardened off. Fertilize more heavily in autumn to build up strength for winter and the following spring. Do not fertilize in spring and then expect delicate ramification.

**Transplanting/Soil** Transplant every two to three years for the majority of trees, yearly for very vigorous trees. Take care to root prune to ensure balanced growth in the roots. Strong roots must be pruned back. In terms of soil, the objective is to be moisture-retentive for summer, but free draining for winter: maples do not like to sit in too much water but must not be allowed to dry out. A mix of 2 parts small particle akadama with 1 part pumice and 1 part lava is a good start. Ensure all dust is removed by sieving from soil.

**Pests/Diseases** Maples are relatively pest and disease free if normal precautions are taken. They are susceptible to a range of non-fatal fungal problems on leaves which can occur after extended periods of wet weather. Keep trees clean and free of fallen leaves, and apply fungicide at the first sign of discolouration or powdery mildew on leaves. Verticillium wilt is a problem for trees in the ground, but generally does not affect trees in pots.

Aphids on fresh tender shoots and scale insects are fairly common problems. An application of systemic pesticide early in the season should be sufficient protection. Check new growth for aphids and spray with contact pesticide if present. Look on the underside of branches for scale insects.

**Pruning/Styling** To build up ramification, pinch the leading tip out from the emerging bud as soon as possible in spring. This will create compact branching and short node length. Defoliating is then possible once the leaves have hardened off, but take care not to weaken the tree too much. For thickness, allow a branch to extend before cutting back to the first node in the future. You can wire young branches at any time: it is best done in spring and then removed when defoliating; alternatively wire in summer and remove it when the leaves drop. The wire can very quickly dig into rapidly thickening branches causing ugly and irreparable scar tissue, so it is essential to remove it before this occurs. Branch pruning is best done immediately after leaf drop in autumn.

**Propagation** Air layering or cuttings from a small leaf-sized parent tree are best. They may be grown from seed but there is natural genetic variation. There is a low success rate with cuttings taken from cultivars that need to be grafted onto stronger root stock.

### Acer buergerianum Trident maple

This widely used variety may become highly ramified and can grow vigorously. Defoliation is possible up to three times a year in a hot climate. It has small three-lobed leaves and grey-orange-brown bark that flakes with age. There are many variations in leaf and node size; look for ones with small leaves and compact branching. It suits most styles and all sizes, and is a popular *shohin* specimen.

**Hardiness/Position** Frost hardy, zones 4–9, but the fleshy roots must be protected from freezing. Young shoots are susceptible to wind and sun burn, so take care in spring and after defoliating if your site is in full sun.

**Watering** Tridents are very thirsty trees when in full sun with lots of foliage. Do not allow to dry out in spring or summer: potentially they need watering twice a day. Do not overwater in winter in case the roots freeze.

**Fertilizing** For trees early in development fertilize heavily from spring until autumn to promote rapid growth. Do not fertilize mature, developed trees until new growth has opened and hardened off.

**Transplanting/Soil** Usually every two to three years with younger trees, and every three to four years with more mature specimens. Small particle soil mix is better for fine root development and water retention.

**Pruning/Styling** Prune secondary branches back to shape immediately after autumn leaf drop. Pinch out the tips of new growth in spring to create compact branching. Defoliate – if desired – once new leaves have hardened off. Wire main branches at an early stage; use a clip-and-grow selective pruning technique to build up secondary and tertiary branching. The tree's vigorous nature means wire can soon become embedded in the branch: act promptly to prevent irreparable scarring.

**Propagation** As for *Acer* above.

### Acer campestre Field maple, hedge maple, common maple

Often collected and used in the UK and Europe. It is vigorous but suffers from large leaves and long, coarse growth which tends to limit it to larger trees. It is difficult to compact and create a delicate shape, so it is more suited for heavy trunk styles. It is often seen with dead wood or hollow trunk features.

### Acer circinatum Vine maple

Native to northwestern North America, very interesting specimens can be found in the understorey of forests, making for unusual trees.

### Acer davidii Snake bark maple

This has large heart-shaped leaves which have fine autumnal colour but do not reduce. The bark is coloured and of great interest. It is rarely seen as bonsai because its growth habit is not suited for ramification.

### Acer ginnala Amur maple

Most tolerant to cold of any maple, this tree may be grown in zone 2, although in a pot winter protection may still be required. It has very deep autumn colours. The leaves are similar to those of the trident maple, although its growth habit tends towards slightly coarser branches. It will flower and then fruit.

### Acer japonicum Full moon maple

A large-leaved variety best suited for larger trees and styles; leaves usually have 9 or 11 lobes, and it often flowers and fruits. Brilliant autumn colouration and winter hardiness are common to the cultivars of *A. japonicum*. It is native to Japan but not as widely used as *A. palmatum* due to its coarser branches.

### Acer monspessulanum Montpellier maple

Similar to the field maple, this is commonly found across Mediterranean Europe. It has three-lobed leaves similar to the trident maple, and it will flower and fruit. Its shrubby growth habit means more compact branching is possible.

### Acer palmatum Japanese maple, mountain maple

Ideally suited for bonsai cultivation, this is a very popular variety. It has delicate branching, a small leaf size and bark that improves with age. The leaves are palmately lobed, and it usually has five pointed lobes. It is generally quite a strong tree but will weaken with age and long-term – 70 years or more – cultivation in a bonsai pot. It is hardy (zones 5–8) but protect from deep frost and freezing temperatures. It suits virtually any style and size. Hundreds of cultivars exist; some are suitable for bonsai, others not. The colours of foliage may vary depending on the level of direct sunlight.

### Acer palmatum 'Arakawa' Rough bark maple

This is grown for the corky rough bark more than the foliage or the branching. It is usually very vigorous and branches tend to be coarse, straight, and youthful compared to the bark, which develops with age. Due to the coarse habit, they tend to make better large upright trees.

### Acer palmatum 'Beni-chidori'

The young foliage is a vibrant red-edged yellow-pink before turning green and giving good autumn colours. Treat it the same as *A. palmatum*, but it is slightly more susceptible to wind damage early in the season.

### Acer palmatum 'Chishio'

This has brilliant blood-red young shoots in spring which turn green and then produce superb autumn colours. It is slow growing but has been supplanted by 'Deshojo' in the bonsai world.

### Acer palmatum 'Deshojo'

This is the queen of spring foliage with intense carmine-red colours in spring. Although it is the hardiest and most vigorous of the red-leaved cultivars, it is still occasionally temperamental and slow for branches to thicken up. Once heavily ramified it can lose vigour if restrained for too many years. As with all cultivars, the cuttings may be unsuccessful in the long term; using young grafted stock is always a better option. When taking air layers, leave for longer to ensure a very healthy root system before separation.

### Acer palmatum 'Kashima' Kashima maple

This is a dwarf *yatsubusa* variety

(cluster of 8 buds) with a different growth habit. It tends to send out multiple branches from one node with multiple branches from the trunk growing out to support a small number of secondary branches. It is difficult to ramify in the same way as other *A. palmatum* cultivars and so adapt techniques accordingly. Buds break very early, often in January, so winter protection is an absolute must to ensure that new foliage does not get damaged by frost. New foliage is a red-lined light yellow-green which is very attractive.

**Acer palmatum 'Katsura' Katsura maple** This is not strictly a dwarf form, but a very small-leaved cultivar with a compact branching structure that makes it suitable for bonsai, although it is not classically used in Japan. It tends to produce multiple branches from the trunk rather than secondary branches from one main branch. The foliage is a vibrant yellow-orange colour.

**Acer palmatum 'Kiyohime'** This dwarf *yatsubusa* cultivar has a horizontal habit and rarely sends up a leader. Lower branches tend to be more vigorous than the apex so take care to maintain apical vigour through regular transplanting. They exhibit the same growth habit as other dwarf cultivars of producing multiple thin branches from the trunk, so lend themselves to a leaf-covered image. Often styled as a broom, but they are best suited to semi-cascade. With great effort, a more classical branch structure can be achieved.

**Acer palmatum 'Kotohime'** Another dwarf *yatsubusa* cultivar which grows in a similar way to the others – although with 'Kotohime' it is possible to develop more obvious branches, and a number of impressive specimens exist with classical bonsai branching structure. Secondary branching tends to be very dense. It can be used to create more upright styles. Responds well to air layering.

**Acer palmatum 'Seigen'** Technically a dwarf variety, this red-leaved cultivar grows in a very similar way to the standard *A. palmatum*. Spring foliage is early and bright red; it is also very susceptible to wind and frost damage so it is best brought out of winter protection late and with care. It tends to be slightly weaker than *A. palmatum* so be conservative with techniques.

**Acer palmatum 'Sharp's Pygmy'** A popular ornamental maple in North America. It has a superb natural dwarf habit similar to 'Kotohime' and 'Shishi-gashira'. The leaves are thicker so tolerate heat better.

**Acer palmatum 'Shishi-gashira'** An ideal species for *shohin* cultivation, 'Shishi-gashira' responds well to air layering and has a very compact growth habit with tiny leaves that tend to curl naturally. It is slow growing but vigorous: plants will thicken over time. The branches and trunk tend to suffer from a lack of taper. It is tolerant of heat and will give deep orange autumn colours.

## *Berberis*
## BARBERRY

This genus of evergreen and deciduous shrubs has around 500 species. It is commonly used in Japan for *shohin* trees and there are a number of larger trees from garden material in the west. A very vigorous grower, berberis tends to sprout all over old wood and withstands drastic pruning, but as it is almost impossible to bend the thick thorny branches it is essential to set the structure early on. Once styled, an almost topiary approach to pruning can be used to keep the tree in shape.
**Hardiness/Position** Frost hardy, zones 4–9, but protect the pot and roots from severe cold (-5°C/23°F). It is happy in full sun or shade.
**Watering** Berberis has moderate drought resistance so take care over summer. Evergreen varieties require more water over winter than deciduous species.
**Fertilizing** Throughout the growing season.
**Transplanting/Soil** Roots are fibrous and will soon fill the pot, so transplanting every two years is recommended. Use a basic small particle soil mix.
**Pests/Diseases** Fungal problems such as powdery mildew, leaf spots, and *Anthracnose* may be a problem for weaker trees or in an infected area, but berberis are generally problem free.
**Pruning/Styling** Prune to shape throughout the growing season. Remove sucker shoots and unwanted branches from the trunk. Wire young shoots and allow them to extend to develop thickness before cutting back.
**Propagation** Seed, cuttings, or air layering.

**Berberis darwinii** A vigorous evergreen shrub originally from South America. It flowers in spring, producing dense racemes of yellow-orange blossoms which then set purple black fruit.

**Berberis thunbergii Japanese barberry** This is a dense deciduous shrub which has pale yellow flowers in mid spring. Red fruits mature in autumn, and stay on the tree throughout the winter months. It is also appreciated for its autumn colours. Japanese barberry is a classical *shohin* species, but it is also suitable for larger trees.

## *Betula*
## BIRCH

This deciduous tree is found all across Eurasia and Northern America. It is suitable for bonsai but suffers from unexpected branch dieback, and the tendency to favour sucker branches over older more ramified branches – which may account for its undeservedly bad reputation in bonsai circles. Styling should account for this and not become dependent on one individual branch. It is appreciated for the silvery bark which comes from years of cultivation in a pot placed in direct sunlight. It is a very vigorous grower and will thicken rapidly in the ground.
**Hardiness/Position** Provide full sun and rotate the tree to ensure even growth. The bark will become silver when exposed to direct sunlight. It is very hardy (zones 3–7), but protect pot and roots from severe cold (-5°C/23°F). It may suffer branch dieback in extreme cold.
**Watering** Do not allow it to dry out from spring to leaf drop. Ease off in winter but do not allow it to dry out.
**Fertilizing** This is a vigorous grower so restrict fertilizer in spring. Wait until growth has stopped in late spring before feeding to build up its strength.
**Transplanting/Soil** Wait until the tree is on the point of bud break before transplanting. Once it is established, do not do any severe root pruning or it may suffer branch loss. Younger trees can be transplanted every other year; leave mature trees slightly longer. Use a basic deciduous soil mix.
**Pests/Diseases** Aphids, leaf spot, and rust may be issues with weaker trees.
**Pruning/Styling** Prune new growth on the external stronger areas back to two or three leaves once growth has finished. Do not touch the internal weaker branches. Defoliation is possible on the external stronger branches to allow sunlight inside. When making hardwood cuts, always ensure that you cut back to a strong viable bud. Prune to leave a small stub above the bud to reduce the risk of dieback. Large pruning scars and trunk chops inevitably lead to dieback. Wire and style in a deciduous fashion with pendulous branches. Branches are flexible when young but they thicken and lignify quickly.
**Propagation** Sow seeds in autumn or take softwood cuttings in spring. Seeds will be of great genetic variance.

**Betula nana Dwarf birch** This deciduous shrub has reddish copper bark. It is very cold hardy and has low tolerance to shade. The small serrated-edged leaves turn golden in autumn.

*Betula pendula* **Silver birch** This deciduous tree is common across the UK and northern Europe. It has arched branches and pendulous branchlets.

*Betula pubescens* **Downy birch** Very similar to *B. pendula*, this tree has slight differences in natural habitat but is identical for bonsai purposes. The downy birch has shoots covered in fine hairs, a slightly duller bark and a finely serrated leaf edge.

## BOUGAINVILLEA
*Bougainvillea*

This genus of flowering vines is found all over the warmer parts of the world from the Mediterranean to Australia. It is a very popular ornamental plant and also species for bonsai due to their vigour, resilience, and reaction to hard pruning.
**Hardiness/Position** Half hardy to frost tender, zone 10. Provide full sun, but provide protection if temperatures fall below 7°C (45°F).
**Watering** Water daily in summer, and more sparingly in winter.
**Fertilizing** Every two weeks throughout the summer months.
**Transplanting/Soil** Every three to four years in spring. Use a free-draining soil mix.
**Pests/Diseases** Red spider mites, mealybugs, aphids, and whiteflies may be troublesome under cover.
**Pruning/Styling** Trim back straggling shoots continually to create a compact plant.
**Propagation** From cuttings.

## BOX
*Buxus*

This evergreen shrub can make very good bonsai if trained correctly, but can be over pruned and create small disconnected foliage pads on the ends of branches. Regular pruning is required to develop trees which can build up foliage mass very quickly. The wood becomes very hard, which means thick branches cannot be bent and carving on *shari* sections is possible. Collected material is available from landscapes and also across southern Europe. Due to the small leaf size, it makes good *shohin* material in any style.
**Hardiness/Position** Frost hardy, zones 5–8. Protect the shrub from frost and cold, drying winds. It will suffer from leaf scorch in intense sun, small pots, and drought conditions.
**Watering** It is thirsty in summer so do not allow it to dry out. It has fleshy roots so do not overwater in winter if there is any chance of freezing.

**Fertilizing** Throughout the growing season.
**Transplanting/Soil** Most plants require transplanting every two years; transplant more mature trees less frequently to maintain a small leaf size. Use a normal deciduous soil mix.
**Pests/Diseases** Red spider mite and box sucker can cause damage to the foliage. Box blight is a fungal disease which starts off as spots on the leaves – which drop off – and soon spreads throughout the tree.
**Pruning/Styling** Defoliation of leaves along the branches, leaving the tip to grow with a few pairs of leaves, will create new shoots at the base of removed leaves. Loosely wire young shoots.
**Propagation** Take cuttings in summer, or propagate by air layering.

*Buxus microphylla* **Japanese box** A slightly less vigorous variety. Several dwarf cultivars exist including 'Kingsville', which is popular across North America.

*Buxus sempervirens* **Common box, European box** This is generally available as hedging or garden material.

## CAMELLIA
*Camellia japonica*

This is an occasionally used species in Japan but not incredibly popular in the West. It is an acid loving evergreen shrub with large waxy leaves and beautiful flowers in winter and spring. There are more than 2,000 cultivars; the best for bonsai have very small single flowers, especially sasanqua varieties.
**Hardiness/Position** Frost hardy, zones 7–9. It is best to protect camellias from frost and drying cold winds. They will grow well in shade or in full sun if watered well.
**Watering** Camellias are thirsty plants in summer: do not allow them to dry out or they will not set flowers.
**Fertilizing** Use an ericaceous fertilizer lightly throughout the growing season. Do not push growth if a compact tree is required.
**Transplanting/Soil** Every two to three years is suitable. Normal bonsai soil mix is good to ensure the pH is neutral.
**Pests/Diseases** Various fungal and viral diseases are possible, although if your plant is healthy and normal precautions are taken it should not be an issue. Yellowing leaves are more likely a sign of nutrient deficiency due to alkaline soil.
**Pruning/Styling** Prune after flowering in spring as flowers tend to set at the end of new growth. Wire and lightly bend woody branches. It is suitable for a number of styles.
**Propagation** Cuttings, layering, seed.

## CHINESE PEA TREE
*Caragana arborescens*

This deciduous shrub from Siberia is occasionally used for *shohin* to medium-sized trees in Asia. A very tough tree, it is tolerates drought, cold, heat, and wind. It is easy to keep and style, and will flower with yellow pea-like blooms that set to pod fruits. It has alternate compound leaves.
**Hardiness/Position** Hardy, zones 2–7. It is tolerant of most conditions but will thrive with a little winter protection.
**Watering** It is drought tolerant but will thrive with regular watering when the surface begins to dry out.
**Fertilizing** Throughout the growing season.
**Transplanting/Soil** Every two to three years depending on the pot size. Use a small particle bonsai mix.
**Pests/Diseases** Generally pest free.
**Pruning/Styling** Prune throughout the year to shape, remove the sucker shoots on the trunk, and wire the branches to shape as normal.
**Propagation** Cuttings, seed.

## HORNBEAM
*Carpinus*

A popular deciduous bonsai, hornbeam has alternate serrated leaves which turn brilliant orange-yellow in autumn. Leaves can become very small with dense ramification. Some varieties will have long pendulous flowers and fruit. The branches do not tend to thicken when grown in a pot, and growth can be in random directions. Regular pruning and wiring will create a more refined structure.
**Hardiness/Position** Frost hardy, zones 4–9. Protect the pot and branches from heavy frost or extended periods of freezing. Give full sun except during intense summer sun when leaves may scorch. Tender new foliage is susceptible to sun and wind burn.
**Watering** Do not allow it to dry out during the growing season, and keep moist but not wet during winter.
**Fertilizing** To push growth begin to fertilize from spring. It does not suffer from elongating node length as much as maples. More refined trees start to develop when leaves have hardened off and been pruned back.
**Transplanting/Soil** Usually every two to three years with younger trees, and three to four with more mature specimens. A small particle soil mix is better for fine root development and water retention.
**Pests/Diseases** Aphids and caterpillars, coral spot, and powdery mildew are possible but it is relatively problem free.
**Pruning/Styling** Allow new shoots to extend out to five or six leaves before pinching out the growing tip. Allow weaker branches to

fully extend as much as they can. Once leaves have hardened off, prune back strong areas, especially the apex and external branches to two leaves, leaving the internal and weaker branches untouched. Prune back to shape as the leaves are dropping. Wire and style young shoots with a loose wiring technique.
**Propagation** Cuttings, seed, air layering.

## *Carpinus betulus* European hornbeam
This is found all across Europe. Some very large trunk collected specimens exist.

## *Carpinus japonica* Japanese hornbeam
This is fast-growing tree that is slower to ramify and build structure due to the large leaf. It is appreciated mainly for its large pendulous catkins.

## *Carpinus turczaninowii* Korean hornbeam
The most commonly used variety for bonsai, imported from Korea and Japan where many large, old thick-trunked collected specimens exist. It is slightly less vigorous but will produce lots of delicate branches.

## *Cedrus*
### CEDAR
This has limited use in bonsai due to the difficulty in getting branches to set, but certain growers have great success. It is an evergreen conifer with needle-like foliage which develops into clusters on short shoots. It is easy to create foliage pads through pruning and basic wiring.
**Hardiness/Position** Hardy tree, zones 5–8, but protect from extreme cold, especially winter winds.
**Watering** It will suffer if overwatered, so allow the soil surface to dry out slightly between watering.
**Fertilizing** Throughout the growing season.
**Transplanting/Soil** Every three to five years into a free-draining conifer mix. Treat the roots with care and be conservative with old soil removal.
**Pests/Diseases** Generally pest free.
**Pruning/Styling** Bend the branches dramatically when the tree is young to create scar tissue and allow the branches to set. Best in upright styles, with single or multiple trunks. The natural growth habit can be weeping. Prune secondary branches to shape rather than over wire.
**Propagation** Seed is best; cuttings have a low success rate.

### *Cedrus atlantica* 'Glauca' Blue Atlas cedar
Probably the best, most widely used cedar, it has beautiful greyish blue foliage.

### *Cedrus brevifolia* Cyprus cedar
This is a slow-growing tree with very short dark green needles.

### *Cedrus deodara* Deodar, Indian cedar
A slow-growing variety with a more pendulous habit and large needles.

### *Cedrus libani* Cedar of Lebanon
This is slow growing with a flat top apex and wide spreading branches.

## *Celastrus orbiculatus*
### ORIENTAL BITTERSWEET
This fruiting vine is often used for *shohin* trees. It is considered an invasive species in eastern parts of North America. It has good autumn colours and the leaf size is quite large. The fruit is an orange-yellow sheath around a vibrant red berry. Ideally plant with a male tree to pollinate the fruit.
**Hardiness/Position** Hardy, zones 4–9. Protect the fruits from light frost, and the tree from heavy frost. Place in full sun except in the heat of summer.
**Watering** Do not allow it to dry out especially when setting fruit; keep moist but not wet in winter.
**Fertilizing** Throughout the growing season but stop when it is setting fruit, then give it a high P:K fertilizer in autumn.
**Transplanting/Soil** Every two to three years; use a moisture-retentive deciduous mix.
**Pests/Diseases** Generally troublefree.
**Pruning/Styling** It will bud on older branches, but it is best to prune back existing branches to shape. Prune back new extensions to a pair of leaves once they grow to five or six leaves. Style into weeping cascade styles according to its natural habit.
**Propagation** Seed, cuttings, layering.

## *Celtis sinensis*
### CHINESE HACKBERRY
This is commonly used in Asia and North America but rarely seen in Europe. It is a very vigorous growing tree, similar in habit to zelkova and Chinese elms. Regular attention and defoliation will enable rapid development of finely ramified, delicate branching. There are many thick-trunked and also abstract Chinese styled trees across the world with well-ramified, angular branching created by clip-and-grow techniques.
**Hardiness/Position** Hardy, zones 5–9, but protect delicate branching from frost damage. Give full sun unless there is extreme heat.
**Watering** Do not allow it to dry out in summer or leaf scorch will occur. It is drought tolerant but prefers to be moist – not wet - in winter.

**Fertilizing** Lightly throughout the growing season unless very regular attention can be given to maintain growth.
**Transplanting/Soil** Every two to three years as the roots begin to fill the pot. Use a deciduous mix.
**Pests/Diseases** Generally pest free.
**Pruning/Styling** Use any deciduous style; it is a versatile tree. Wire and shape the main and secondary branches, then build up ramification through regular defoliation and the clip-and-grow technique. It is very important to maintain regular branch division of two to every node, as Chinese hackberry tends to send out multiple branches from one node. Aim to create a delicate twig structure by thinning these out to two healthy shoots.
**Propagation** Cuttings, seed, layering.

## *Chaenomeles*
### FLOWERING QUINCE
A flowering shrub native to East Asia, it is widely used for bonsai. There are a number of different coloured cultivars; choose one with small leaves and small flowers for best results. With the exception of 'Chojubai' it is generally seen in clump styles.

*Chaenomeles* is a member of the rose family, so there are two areas of great concern. Do not allow too many sucker shoots to develop on young trees – and none at all on older trees – because it may cause established branches to weaken and die. 'Chojubai' especially are susceptible to bacterial infection, especially in the roots so it is a good idea to sterilize tools before and after pruning, and essential to treat large wounds with antibacterial wound sealant. Crown gall disease is a knobbly growth in the roots that will spread to the branches and ultimately kill the tree if left uncontrolled. To prevent it, always use fresh soil and transplant in autumn once temperatures start to drop. If it is present, remove and destroy all galls and soil, soak the rootball in an Agromycin bath for several hours and plant into fresh soil. Treat the soil with Agromycin every couple of months and allow the tree to put on healthy growth. Crown gall mainly affects older and weaker trees; it cannot be cured, but it can be managed.
**Hardiness/Position** Frost hardy, zones 5–9. Some varieties will need a cold period in order to set flowers. Protect it from intense midsummer heat, but otherwise give full sun.
**Watering** Do not allow it to dry out. 'Chojubai' especially will drop leaves if they are water stressed. Keep it moist but not wet in winter.
**Fertilizing** Regularly throughout the growing season except when flowering. The exception is 'Chojubai', which can be fertilized all season.

**Transplanting/Soil** Best transplanted in autumn; see notes above. Use a moisture-retentive akadama-rich mix to help develop its fine roots.
**Pests/Diseases** Aphids on fresh tender growth, and crown gall can be a problem. It will drop leaves if strong chemicals are used.
**Pruning/Styling** Generally clump styles are used, except for 'Chojubai', which are often seen as in single-trunk cascade, windswept, or slanting styles. Allow the shoots to extend, and pinch out tips before allowing the growth to harden off; then prune back into shape.
**Propagation** Cuttings are very successful.

***Chaenomeles japonica* 'Chojubai'** This is most common in the *shohin* world, and is a very versatile and popular small-leaved variety with delicate red flowers. It flowers throughout autumn, winter, and spring. Defoliation to promote ramification is possible, but it will weaken the tree. There are several varieties in the bonsai world; some ramify well but flower poorly, while others flower profusely and ramify poorly.

***Chaenomeles speciosa* Flowering quince** A number of cultivars exist of this deciduous flowering shrub; 'Toyo-nishiki' is a multicoloured variety popular in Japan. Generally the clump style is used. This has a larger oval leaf.

## *Chamaecyparis*
## CYPRESS, FALSE CYPRESS

This fairly common coniferous tree is often seen as bonsai, although it can be difficult to maintain the foliage pads. Garden centre material is often used, but take care that the root system is suitable for a bonsai pot. Foliage management is key, as adventitious budding is very rare. Scale foliage grows out in fans, and needs to be restricted carefully. Prune out the strongest growing tip only if the foliage behind it has light green growing tips as well. If all growing tips are removed, the branches will die. When styling, spread the foliage out and give it space to grow into. Internal branches will yellow and die from lack of sunlight.
**Hardiness/Position** Hardy, zones 4–9. It is cold tolerant but protect the pot from hard frost or extended freezing. Keep it sheltered from cold drying winds. Provide full sun in summer.
**Watering** Unlike other conifers, it is not drought tolerant. Do not allow it to dry out; it is a thirsty tree.
**Fertilizing** Throughout the growing season.
**Transplanting/Soil** Every two to three years for younger trees, but longer for mature

specimens where maintaining the image is the goal.
**Pests/Diseases** Spider mites can be an issue.
**Pruning/Styling** Foliage management is the key point. Wire and style the main branches but do not over wire the foliage. They are generally upright trees as this is their natural growth habit.
**Propagation** Cuttings, seed.

***Chamaecyparis obtusa* Hinoki cypress** This is most commonly used and found across Japan. Several dwarf cultivars exist. They have bluish green on the underside of their foliage.

***Chamaecyparis pisifera* Sawara cypress** 'Boulevard' and 'Plumosa' cultivars are easily available. They have a white underside to their foliage.

## *Cornus*
## DOGWOOD

This flowering deciduous tree is occasionally used for its interesting flowers. It is difficult to ramify and create into a maple-like tree, and the branches tend towards the coarse or lack taper, although it is worth persevering for the seasonal interest they provide.
**Hardiness/Position** Frost hardy, zones 5–9, but protect delicate branching from frost damage. Provide full sun unless periods of extreme heat occur.
**Watering** Do not allow it to dry out through the growing season, and keep it moist but not wet in winter.
**Fertilizing** Heavily after flowering, stop during flowering, and then lightly throughout the rest of the growing season.
**Transplanting/Soil** Every two to three years for younger trees, but longer for mature specimens where maintaining the image is the goal.
**Pests/Diseases** Generally pest free.
**Pruning/Styling** Use deciduous styles, and treat in a similar way to maple, but do not defoliate. The best way to achieve more flowers is to encourage more branches.
**Propagation** Cuttings, layering, seed.

***Cornus kousa* Kousa dogwood** Lots of white flowers in early summer turning to large red fruit and large leaves which turn deep orange and red in autumn. Very strong and pest resistant.

***Cornus mas* European cherry, cornelian cherry** This is found across Southern Europe. It flowers in late winter and spring with small yellow flowers followed by red cherry-like fruits.

***Cornus officinalis* Japanese cornelian cherry** This has clusters of yellow flowers in late winter and spring followed by red berries.

## *Corylopsis*
## WINTER HAZEL

This winter-flowering deciduous tree is grown mainly for the flowers. It is mostly seen as clump styles although single trunk trees are also possible. Many branches are desirable in order to appreciate the flowers. It is an acid-loving plant so use an ericaceous feed if the leaves turn yellow. Cultivate as for *Cornus*.

## *Cotoneaster*
## COTONEASTER

This is very versatile and a suitable shrub for bonsai with more than 200 different varieties, both evergreen and deciduous. It is a good beginner tree as it is forgiving and can be easily clipped into shape. With careful cultivation, great results can be achieved, especially with *shohin*-sized trees. Small foliage, flowers, and fruit are the main character points. Material can be obtained from gardens and cut back dramatically, as they bud from old wood.
**Hardiness/Position** Hardy, zones 4–9, but remember to provide additional protection when grown in pots. Give full sun but protect the fruit from birds when it has set.
**Watering** Cotoneaster is drought tolerant but will thrive if watered regularly. Do not allow it to dry out when flowering or setting fruit.
**Fertilizing** Apply lightly throughout the growing season except during flowering. It does not respond to heavy fertilizing.
**Transplanting/Soil** Every two to three years for younger specimens; longer for mature trees where maintaining the image is the goal.
**Pests/Diseases** Generally pest free.
**Pruning/Styling** Wire the main branches and the larger secondary ones. Prune to shape the foliage pads. Allow spring extensions and then cut back to shape. Defoliation will increase ramification but only once the leaves have hardened off, and if there is enough time left in the season to grow and harden off again before any frost. Any style is possible but they are often seen as cascade or windswept due to their natural growth habit.
**Propagation** Take cuttings or sow seed.

***Cotoneaster adpressus*** This deciduous variety has pink flowers in spring, red berries and then autumn foliage which drops.

***Cotoneaster horizontalis* Rockspray cotoneaster** The flowers can be pink/white followed by red berries. It is also deciduous.

***Cotoneaster microphyllus*** This variety is evergreen with small leaves.

## *Crassula ovata*
### JADE TREE, MONEY TREE

This is native to South Africa and is suited to hot climates, or indoor cultivation. Technically it is not a tree, but a succulent plant. It is ideal as a low-maintenance indoor tree.

**Hardiness/Position** Frost tender, zone 10. Do not subject to temperatures below 5°C (41°F). Full sun is best. If it is grown indoors then close to a window is best.

**Watering** Crassulas store water in their leaves and have adapted for life in arid conditions. Allow your tree to dry out between waterings. Overwatering causes terminal root issues.

**Fertilizing** Very little is required; once a month from spring to autumn.

**Transplanting/Soil** Crassula requires a fast draining non water-retentive soil mixture every two to three years.

**Pests/Diseases** Generally pest free.

**Pruning/Styling** Wiring is difficult, but pruning is sufficient. If you do wire, remember that the branches are brittle and snap easily. Do not seal any wounds. Style into upright or clump styles.

**Propagation** Cuttings, even from a single leaf will be successful.

## *Crataegus*
### HAWTHORN

This deciduous tree flowers and fruits, and is especially popular in the UK where native specimens are collected from the wild or the garden. It has spiky branches which have a natural angular growth habit and a tendency to grow multiple shoots from one node.

**Hardiness/Position** Hardy, zones 4–8. Protect it from hard, prolonged frosts. Provide full sun and a well-ventilated place in the garden. Do not place it close to *Juniperus* species.

**Watering** Do not allow it to dry out in summer or leaf scorch will occur. Keep it moist but not wet in winter.

**Fertilizing** Apply throughout the growing season, stop when it is flowering, then start again with a high P:K preparation when the fruit is set.

**Transplanting/Soil** Every three to four years into a deciduous mix. It tends to sulk when the roots are pruned, so be conservative with transplanting. Leaving mature trees to become slightly pot-bound will result in increased flowering.

**Pests/Diseases** Fungal problems are the biggest concern. Cedar rusts and fireblight are an issue and will spread to *Juniperus* and vice versa. Any signs of rust must be dealt with

by regular applications of various fungicides and destruction of infected material.

**Pruning/Styling** The natural growth habit can result in some chaotic but wild and beautiful branching. This can be recreated and improved by taking a clip-and-grow approach to the secondary branching. Do not wire the branches and put curves in them; think of the branches as a series of connected straight lines. Allow new growth to extend before pruning the growing tip off. Allow the foliage to harden off before pruning strong areas back to one or two nodes. Allow the weaker areas more foliage to build up strength. Younger branches may be wired. Dead wood features are possible. Suits any style other than broom.

**Propagation** Cuttings, seed.

***Crataegus cuneata*** **Japanese hawthorn** This has oval leaves, white flowers in late spring, and large rosehip style fruits. It is more delicate than *C. monogyna*.

***Crataegus laevigata*** **'Paul's Scarlet'** This double-flowered scarlet cultivar is often used for bonsai. It rarely fruits.

***Crataegus monogyna*** **Common hawthorn** This has smaller white flowers followed by small red fruit in autumn. It is one of the best varieties for bonsai in the UK with some superb natural specimens available.

## *Cryptomeria japonica*
### JAPANESE CEDAR

This evergreen coniferous tree has needle-like foliage and red bark. Style them only as formal upright trees or as formal uprights on rock.

**Hardiness/Position** Hardy, zones 5–9. Protect the pot from extended freezing. The foliage may turn brown after frost, but this is normal. Give full sun and a well-ventilated position.

**Watering** Do not allow it to dry out although it is slightly drought tolerant.

**Fertilizing** Throughout the growing season.

**Transplanting/Soil** Every three to four years, but longer for mature specimens. Wait until the foliage is beginning to push.

**Pests/Diseases** Red spider mites can be an issue in dense trees. Mist the underside of foliage to prevent infestations.

**Pruning/Styling** Prune back the stems of strong growing tips to restrict growth, but only if neighbouring shoots have live growing tips as well. It will send out adventitious buds readily if it is healthy. Ensure that there is space between the branches so sunlight and wind can penetrate the tree. Wire the main branches and lignified secondary shoots. It

has a very distinct natural growth habit so do not deviate from that.

**Propagation** Sow seed or take cuttings.

## *Diospyros*
### PERSIMMON, EBONY

This is a widely used genus in the tropical regions, with some in temperate climates. There is a wide range of deciduous and evergreen trees and shrubs with more than 500 species. Treat it in a similar way to most deciduous trees.

***Diospyros kaki*** **Kaki persimmon** This has large edible orange fruits. Branching is coarse and leaves are large so it is limited to large trees, usually literati. It is a very evocative autumnal image for the Japanese.

***Diospyros rhombifolia*** **Princess persimmon** This is a very popular fruiting variety in Japan and is starting across the West. Its growth habit means structurally the trees lack great interest but they become covered in fruit in autumn. A male tree is needed to ensure a good crop of fruit. It will propagate from branch and root cuttings easily.

***Diospyros whyteana*** **Wild coffee** Native to South Africa, this has glossy leaves and creamy fragrant flowers which fruit.

***Diospyros ferrea*** **Black ebony, Philippine ebony, persimmon** This is used across SE Asia, particularly in Taiwan.

## *Ehretia microphylla*
### FUKIEN TEA

Also known as *Carmona microphylla*, this is generally considered an indoor tree, that is widely available as a starter bonsai around the world. It can be temperamental, given unfavourable conditions. White flowers are followed by small black berries.

**Hardiness/Position** Frost tender, zones 10–11. Growing indoors or in a greenhouse will give best results. If it is grown indoors, a south- or west-facing window is best, ideally with 4 to 6 hours of light a day. Provide protection once temperatures drop below 13°C/55°F.

**Watering** Do not allow it to dry out at any time of year, and water it as and when the soil surface starts to dry out.

**Fertilizing** Year round, less during winter. A liquid fertilizer is easiest once or twice a month when growing indoors.

**Transplanting/Soil** Once every two years. Use moisture-retentive easy care bonsai soil mix.

**Pests/Diseases** Aphids, scale insects, and

mealybugs may be a problem but it is generally trouble free. Flowers can attract insects in warmer climates. Foliage problems are most likely due to poor soil or overwatering.

**Pruning/Styling** Foliage pads respond to topiary-style pruning, but for improvement, thin out branches and apply a clip-and-grow technique throughout the growing season. Wire the main branches if necessary.

**Propagation** Take cuttings in spring/summer or sow seed.

## Elaeagnus
### ELEAGNUS

This shrub is well suited for bonsai, and responds well to defoliation and styling. They are fast-growing and vigorous plants, tolerant of many conditions. They have small flowers followed by pendulous fruit, and are suited for a variety of styles and sizes. The leaves are dark green with a silvery underside. They will reduce with defoliation.

**Hardiness/Position** Hardy, zones 4–8. Protect the pot from extended freezing. Full sun and a windy position are no problem throughout the year.

**Watering** It is drought tolerant but will thrive if kept moist throughout the year.

**Fertilizing** Do this throughout the growing season, with a break during flowering.

**Transplanting/Soil** Every two to three years into a deciduous mix.

**Pests/Diseases** Generally pest free.

**Pruning/Styling** Allow new growth to extend to five or six leaves before pruning back to two leaves. Defoliation is possible once the leaves become hard. Wiring is no problem. The branches can become too coarse so thin out strong areas regularly to stop it happening, especially on small trees. Use any style except broom, and any size but small to medium is best.

**Propagation** Cuttings.

*Elaeagnus multiflora* This is a deciduous shrub, with small flowers and red fruits.

*Elaeagnus pungens* **Thorny elaeagnus** This evergreen shrub has flowers in summer followed by beige coloured fruit.

## Euonymus
### SPINDLE TREE

This deciduous tree is renowned for its vivid autumnal colours and fruit. It is relatively easy to keep, well suited for smaller size trees due to the small fruit and leaf size.

**Hardiness/Position** Hardy, zones 4–8. Protect the pot from freezing. Provide full sun but

shade the tree in intense sunlight.

**Watering** It is a thirsty tree, so do not allow it to dry out in the growing season.

**Fertilizing** Throughout the growing season once new growth has been stopped.

**Transplanting/Soil** Do this every two to three years into a deciduous mix.

**Pests/Diseases** Generally pest free.

**Pruning/Styling** Use deciduous styling; it tends to send out multiple shoots from one node so ensure these are not allowed to thicken. Prune it to shape and wire as required. It is similar to other deciduous trees.

**Propagation** Seed, cuttings.

*Euonymus alatus* **Winged spindle** This has beautiful autumnal colours and corky, winged bark which develops on branches. It produces small orange/red fruit in autumn.

*Euonymus europaeus* **European spindle** This has pink flowers followed by red seed capsules.

*Euonymus sieboldianus* **Japanese spindle** This tree produces pink or white fruit and is a very vigorous grower.

## Fagus
### BEECH

This deciduous tree makes a striking bonsai image. The two main species are European and Japanese, although there are some variants on those. An apically dominant tree, work must be done to restrict strong upward and outward growth or suffer a loss of internal branches. The lower branches are slow to thicken, and the upper branches are quick to become coarse. They are generally very upright styles and occasionally groups. Medium to large size is best.

**Hardiness/Position** Hardy, zones 4–9. They are winter hardy, but protect the pot from deep freeze. Give full sun except in extreme conditions, and protect new shoots from wind/sun burn.

**Watering** As with other deciduous trees, do not allow it to dry out in summer. Keep it moist but not wet in winter.

**Fertilizing** Do this with younger trees from bud break throughout the season. For more mature, refined specimens, wait until after pruning and for leaves to harden off before fertilizing. Fertilize more heavily in autumn.

**Transplanting/Soil** Every two years for younger trees, every three to four for older specimens with an established root system. Beech have a tendency to develop one or two very strong roots. These need to be pruned back strongly in favour of weaker side roots, which should be left unpruned to grow. Any

strong growth should be cut back in favour of fibrous roots or uneven surface roots and branching will develop. Use a deciduous soil mix, with small particle size.

**Pests/Diseases** Aphids, beech bark scale and powdery mildew are potentially a problem but it is generally trouble free.

**Pruning/Styling** Stop new growth from extending on strong areas by pinching out the terminal growth to leave only one or two leaves. Weaker internal areas should be allowed to fully extend to six or seven leaves before stopping terminal growth. Prune it back to shape in autumn after leaf drop. Prune back to the first or second node. Allowing extension will increase the leaf size and node length, so balance the shaping requirements with energy requirements. In autumn, prune back any strong branches and also prune to shape, giving consideration to bud orientation. Wire the tree in winter or late summer. The clip-and-grow technique is very successful for ramification. Do not defoliate.

**Propagation** Seed, or air layering in early summer.

*Fagus crenata* **Japanese beech** This commonly imported variety tends to hold onto its bronze autumnal foliage throughout winter as protection for the buds. The trunk can be almost white.

*Fagus sylvatica* **European beech** Many different cultivars are available; choose small or interesting leaves. It usually drops its leaves.

## Ficus
### FIG

Widely used in warmer and tropical climates, figs are often indoor plants across northern Europe and North America. There are more than 800 species, with many suitable for bonsai. It tolerates hard pruning and will bud from older wood. It is difficult to bend heavier branches, so set the structure early. They thrive in good conditions, so will need warmth and light if used as an indoor plant.

**Hardiness/Position** Frost tender, zones 10–11. Keep them inside if temperatures drop below 15°C (60°F). Protect them from cold wind. Direct sunlight is best for encouraging small foliage, although they will tolerate lower light levels. Do not overheat them in summer. High humidity levels are best, so a gravel tray can help.

**Watering** Keep them moist for best results. Do not allow them to dry out dramatically or stay waterlogged.

**Fertilizing** Lightly throughout the growing season.

**Transplanting/Soil** Every two to three years in spring. Use a moisture-retentive mix.
**Pests/Diseases** They are generally problem free, although scale can be an issue. Leaf discolouration or drop is generally caused by poor positioning.
**Pruning/Styling** Prune to shape, and thin out dense areas. Defoliation is possible on strong trees. Wire thinner shoots to style. Clip-and-grow is a good technique to use. A lot of trees tend to end up with very upward growing branches so take care to lower them or prune to favour downward growing shoots. Use any style, and any size.
**Propagation** Take cuttings.

*Ficus benjamina* **Weeping fig** Tender evergreen usually considered an indoor tree in temperate climates.

*Ficus macrophylla* **Moreton Bay fig** Tender evergreen with a mature buttressed trunk which may prefer an indoor position in temperate climates.

*Ficus platypoda* **Australian fig** Commonly used in Australia, this tender evergreen has smooth leaves and small orange-red flowers.

*Ficus retusa* **Banyan fig** This has distinctive aerial roots which should be encouraged, but also pruned if they are becoming too thick and out of balance.

*Ficus rubiginosa* **Port Jackson fig** Tender evergreen with glossy dark green leaves.

*Ficus salicifolia* **Willow leaf fig** Also known as *F. neriifolia*, this species is widely used due to the very small, thin leaf shape that makes it ideal for bonsai.

## *Ginkgo biloba*
## MAIDENHAIR TREE
This unique deciduous tree has no living relatives. It has unusual foliage that turns golden in autumn. It has a unique growth habit and should be styled as such. It is best to stick to narrow upright growth and multiple stems coming from the trunk. Any other styling looks forced and artificial. Ramification and creating a traditional deciduous branching structure are difficult.
**Hardiness/Position** Hardy, zones 4–10, but protect the pot from freezing as the roots are fleshy. Give full sun except in extreme heat.
**Watering** Do not allow it to dry out in the growing season and keep it moist but not wet in winter.

**Fertilizing** Lightly during the growing season; it is a slow grower and cannot be forced.
**Transplanting/Soil** Transplant every two to three years, or slightly longer for more mature trees. Use a deciduous mix.
**Pests/Diseases** Generally pest free.
**Pruning/Styling** See above. Trim back shoots in autumn. Branches should be upswept.
**Propagation** Seed, layering.

## *Ilex serrata*
## JAPANESE DECIDUOUS HOLLY, WINTERBERRY
The grey bark, thin slightly serrated leaves and red autumn-winter fruit make this a good species to work with for bonsai. It flowers in late spring; females need to be close to a male tree to pollinate and fruit. Once the berries have set and the leaves are starting to change colour, protect it from birds. The branches are slow to thicken and growth tends to happen very vertically. Prune it back and favour downward growing shoots.
**Hardiness/Position** Frost hardy, zones 5–9; protect from heavy frosts. Give slight shade in the midsummer sun; otherwise give full sun.
**Watering** Do not allow holly to dry out in the growing season, especially if it is fruiting. It will soon lose its fruit. It suits wetter climates.
**Fertilizing** Fertilize lightly throughout the year. If vegetative growth is required, fertilize heavily; if fruits are required, fertilize lightly and then once fruit has set, apply a high p-k fertilizer for late summer and autumn.
**Transplanting/Soil** Every two to three years in spring. Use a deciduous mix.
**Pests/Diseases** Aphids can be a problem on younger shoots.
**Pruning/Styling** Clump and informal upright styles are best. Allow new growth to extend to four or five leaves before wiring it down and pinching out the terminal growth. Once leaves have hardened off – or in autumn – prune it back to shape. Consider the position and direction of the buds when pruning; favour outward and horizontal or downward buds if possible.
**Propagation** From seed, or by layering.

## *Jasminum nudiflorum*
## WINTER-FLOWERING JASMINE
Often used for *shohin* trees, this has beautiful yellow flowers in the middle of winter. Relatively easy to keep, it will bud on older wood. It is slightly difficult to maintain old branches for a long time but it responds well to defoliation. Suits any style, but it is often seen as semi- or full cascade.
**Hardiness/Position** Frost hardy, zones 6–9. Smaller trees need protection from freezing.

Give it full sun, but provide shade in intense midsummer heat.
**Watering** Do not allow it to dry out in the growing season; keep moist, but not wet, in winter.
**Fertilizing** Apply a little throughout the growing season.
**Transplanting/Soil** Every two to three years as a guideline, in a very small pot potentially annually. Use a small particle water-retentive deciduous mix.
**Pests/Diseases** Generally pest free.
**Pruning/Styling** Allow the growth to extend before pruning it back to shape. Jasmine is a vigorous grower and will bud from old wood. Thin out dense congested branches. Wire the main branches as and when required. Ramification can develop quickly through pruning, clip-and-grow, and defoliation.
**Propagation** Cuttings, layering.

## *Juniperus*
## JUNIPER
Versatile and full of character, this is one of the most popular choices for bonsai cultivation. Many species are available, and collected *yamadori* specimens are highly sought after. Two types, scale and needle junipers, have different growth and cultivation characteristics. Foliage management is very important with junipers; never remove large amounts of foliage at one time – it is the driving force behind the tree. Without foliage, the tree will stall, suffer, and potentially die. With correct cultivation, junipers develop rapidly and create beautiful trees. Dead wood features are especially beautiful and characteristic of junipers, which have evolved to grow in the harshest of wild environments.
**Hardiness/Position** Hardy, zones 3 to 11 depending on the species. They withstand a wide range of temperatures but protect small trees in winter and pots from hard, long freezes. Position in full sun unless it is very intense or if the tree is slightly weaker, when slight shade is better. Keeping junipers in shade causes the foliage to elongate and turn dark green. Keep them away from hawthorns, both natural or bonsai.
**Watering** They are generally drought tolerant but will thrive if kept moist year round. Avoid overwatering, but do not allow the soil to dry out. Keep needle junipers much more moist.
**Fertilizing** Apply regularly throughout the growing season.
**Transplanting/Soil** Do this every two to three years as a younger tree or *shohin*. For larger and more established trees, wait as long as possible – provided water can penetrate the surface easily and the tree shows no signs of ill health. The roots are very fine so a small

particle conifer mix is best. Charcoal is often a good addition to the soil mix depending on the water quality. Transplant in spring; needle junipers should be transplanted late in the season once the temperature has started to rise, usually early May in the UK.

**Pests/Diseases** Spider mites attack the foliage from the underside and inside out. The foliage will begin to go off colour, then yellow and die. Misting the underside regularly helps prevent this. Spray with pesticide if it is infected – twice within a week if necessary.

Fungal infections can be a serious issue in some parts of the world. Cedar-hawthorn rust and juniper tip blight can seriously damage trees. Regular application of fungicides in the growing season, sterilization of tools, and destruction of infected material is essential for stopping the spread. It will attack the weakest trees first.

**Pruning/Styling** Juniper is suitable for very dramatic styles. The branches and trunk are flexible and tolerate some damage. Create movement and compact foliage pads close to the trunk wherever possible. Foliage management is essential. Allow growth to extend before cutting out the central stem of the most vigorous shoot, but only if there are shoots with active light green growing tips behind it to continue the growth. Removing too much foliage – particularly if it is actively growing foliage – causes a flush of undesirable juvenile growth that looks quite different from adult growth, so never remove more than 40 per cent of the foliage in one go (*see also pp.117 and 174–175*). Multiple shoots from one node will need thinning out.

**Propagation** Take cuttings; layering is possible but slow.

### *Juniperus californica* California juniper
As the name suggests, this is native to California. Tolerant of extreme drought and heat, it thrives in good soil and regular watering. It is often collected with very thin live veins on heavily weathered and hard dead wood.

### *Juniperus chinensis*
This is the most popular bonsai juniper imported from Japan or cultivated in the West. It is a very versatile tree with a number of different foliage types, which make it more or less suitable for certain styles.

### *Juniperus chinensis* 'Blaauw'
This is commonly available garden material: if you are going to use a garden variety, choose this one. It has tight compact foliage and a suitable growth habit.

### *Juniperus chinensis* 'Itoigawa'
is a dense, small leaved light green type that sends out longer shoots. It is ideally suited for *shohin*-sized trees. It will suffer in extreme heat due to the larger surface area of thinner foliage, leading to higher moisture loss.

### *Juniperus chinensis* 'Kishu'
has a slightly bluey foliage that is coarser and tends to form pompom-like 360-degree growth. This can be avoided by removing downward growing foliage. It suits hot climates and larger trees.

### *Juniperus chinensis* 'San Jose'
Another commonly available bonsai/garden species. Its growth habit is very different in that it is generally juvenile foliage and there is an incredible tendency to send multiple shoots from one node. The systematic removal of all of them will result in more juvenile foliage creating a vicious circle. Allow more branches to develop and take a conservative approach to foliage removal and transplanting. Let the tree mature and keep heavy pruning to a minimum. Remove dead and weak foliage from the inside of foliage pads on a regular basis.

### *Juniperus communis* Common juniper
This is difficult – but not impossible – to cultivate as bonsai. It has needle foliage that needs pinching back in a similar way to the scale junipers. It loves moist, water-retentive soils and is most successful in very wet climates. Be conservative and careful with all work and leave lots of strong foliage on the tree.

### *Juniperus occidentalis* Western juniper, sierra juniper
Native to western North America, it has quite bluish foliage, which tends to be quite juvenile and coarse during the early stages of development but will mature into more compact scale foliage over time. It benefits from becoming slightly pot-bound. Collected specimens are available.

### *Juniperus procumbens*
A few cultivars exist, including 'Nana', which are suitable for bonsai. Treat them similarly to *J. chinensis* 'San Jose'.

### *Juniperus rigida* Needle juniper
This Japanese variety has prickly and delicate foliage, and will need wiring to prevent it from sagging. Pinching out new growth will cause adventitious budding on healthy trees. It thrives in warm climates but tends to struggle in northern Europe. It is a thirsty and hungry plant.

### *Juniperus sabina* Sabina juniper, Savin's juniper
This is commonly collected throughout Europe, and many cultivars exist for garden use. Collected trees can make very good bonsai although trunks and dead wood tend to be smaller and softer than other species. The foliage quality varies with location as with all collected varieties. Careful management of foliage is essential for success.

### *Juniperus scopulorum* Rocky Mountain juniper
A native of western North America, collected trees show incredible dead wood features, and superb movement and character. The foliage needs similar care to the western juniper; strike a careful balance between selective pruning and letting it grow.

## *Lagerstroemia indica*
### CRAPE MYRTLE
This deciduous tree flowers in late summer, has a distinctive smooth bark and thrives in warmer weather.

**Hardiness/Position** Frost tender, zones 7–9. Provide protection if temperatures fall below 5ºC (40ºF). Position in full sun in summer, and slight shade in extreme heat.

**Watering** This is a thirsty tree, especially when it is in flower. Do not allow it to dry out in the growing season. Keep it moist but not wet in winter.

**Fertilizing** Apply lightly before flowering, stop during flowering, then fertilize heavily after flowering.

**Transplanting/Soil** Transplant every two to three years in spring, but wait longer for more mature trees. Use a deciduous mix.

**Pests/Diseases** Generally pest free but it can get aphids on new shoots.

**Pruning/Styling** As with other deciduous trees. The branches are brittle so bend them only when young. Allow shoots to extend in spring to six or seven leaves and then prune them back to two. Flowers will then set before blossoming in summer. It produces many vertically growing shoots which should be pruned off as early as possible.

**Propagation** Seed, cuttings.

## *Larix*
### LARCH
Flexible and relatively fast growing, these upright deciduous conifers have great character and are ideal for bonsai. The young foliage is attractive, as is the autumnal colour. The bark quality on older trees is superb.

**Hardiness/Position** Hardy, zones 3–8, but protect the roots from heavy freezing. The foliage will burn in midsummer heat so keep it in semi shade.

**Watering** Keep it moist during the growing season, and slightly drier over winter.

**Fertilizing** Do not fertilize until growth has been stopped, or branching could become too coarse. Fertilize heavily in autumn.
**Transplanting/Soil** Every two to three years is best; do not allow larch to become too pot-bound. Timing is key: it is best done just as the buds are starting to swell but before they break. Avoid heavily root pruning established trees. Use a standard coniferous mix.
**Pests/Diseases** Generally pest free.
**Pruning/Styling** Allow new growth to extend further than the overall shape before pruning off the terminal growth. Prune to shape in late summer. Structural pruning can be done after leaf drop and before spring. Branches have a tendency to become coarse, so thinning them out is necessary. Wire the tree in winter or spring, but be aware that branches thicken quickly and wire can dig in if care is not taken.
**Propagation** From seed or cuttings.

*Larix decidua* **European larch** Collected specimens of this delicately branching tree often originate from the European Alps.

*Larix kaempferi* **Japanese larch** This is a very vigorous grower, and the branches soon become coarse. It thickens quickly. It is a good starter tree but is also of interest to advanced bonsai growers. It is a forestry tree in the UK and collected trees are available.

*Larix laricina* **American larch** A cold hardy tree suitable for the northernmost parts of North America. Collected trees have superb character, but grow slowly in cold climates.

## *Malus*
## CRAB APPLE

These are very good flowering and fruiting bonsai but make for difficult ramification and branching structure. Older branches tend to die or become very difficult to create a tapered shape. They are however very beautiful when flowering and in fruit, so it is worth cultivating them. It is generally easy to create fruit in a normal garden or rural setting. To increase your chances of success, have two different varieties flowering close to each other. Many different varieties are available: choose ones with small fruit for bonsai.
**Hardiness/Position** Frost hardy, zones 4–9. Protect from deep freezes especially if it is in a small or shallow pot. Position in full sun except in extreme heat.
**Watering** Do not allow crab apples to dry out, especially when flowering or in fruit. Keep them moist but not wet in winter.
**Fertilizing** Apply lightly in early spring, pause for flowering and fruit setting; lightly

afterwards once fruit have set in midsummer; and then fertilize heavily in autumn.
**Transplanting/Soil** Every two to three years, taking care to balance the growth. Use an akadama-heavy mix or something that holds moisture and nutrients well.
**Pests/Diseases** Aphids, woolly aphids, and caterpillars are an issue but fungal problems such as apple scab, canker, or fireblight are more of a concern. Investigate strange growths or heavily discoloured leaves immediately.
**Pruning/Styling** Depending on the objective, allow new growth to develop thickness and length, or prune it back quickly to create compact branching, and develop flower buds close to the tree. Prune back by late summer in order to set some flowers for the following year. Wire the branches carefully but look more towards achieving healthy growth and pruning back to create movement in branches, rather than over wiring. There are various styles and size, although consider the fruit size for smaller trees.
**Propagation** From seed, layering, or cuttings.

*Malus cerasifera* **Nagasaki crab apple** This is one of the most popular species for bonsai; it is a prolific flowering tree with pink flower buds that open to white flowers. It produces small red round fruit in autumn.

*Malus halliana* **Hall's crab apple** Bears pink flowers and small purple fruit.

*Malus sieboldii* **Decorative crab apple** Also known as *M. toringo*, it produces tiny fruit, and is suitable for smaller *shohin* trees.

*Malus sylvestris* **Common crab apple** White or pink blossoms are followed by yellow-green or red-flushed fruit.

## *Metasequoia glyptostroboides*
## DAWN REDWOOD

This deciduous conifer has a very vertical growth habit. Treat the delicate fronds with care when wiring. Pinch back new growth and it will send out many adventitious buds. Train it only in a formal upright style with downward sweeping, straightish branches.
**Hardiness/Position** Frost hardy, zones 5–8. Protect it from deep freezing conditions and intense sunlight: the delicate foliage may burn if the soil dries out.
**Watering** Do not allow it to dry out in hot weather; keep it moist in the growing season.
**Fertilizing** It is a very vigorous grower, so little fertilizer is required unless you are pushing growth.
**Transplanting/Soil** Transplant every two to

three years, and aim to develop a spreading, even root base. Use a moisture-retentive coniferous mix.
**Pests/Diseases** Generally pest free.
**Pruning/Styling** Pinch out terminal growth if you are looking to ramify or keep compact. It has a pyramidal growth habit so wire the branches downwards for a mature effect.
**Propagation** Cuttings, seed.

## *Myrtus communis*
## MYRTLE

This evergreen shrub or small tree is common in the Mediterranean where it is collected for bonsai. Cultivated material is also available. It will tolerate very hard pruning and back buds very well. It has fragrant flowers in summer and will set small black edible fruit. It is a hermaphrodite tree so pollinates easily.
**Hardiness/Position** Frost tender, zones 8–11. Protect it from temperatures below 5°C (40°F). Position it in full sun.
**Watering** It is drought tolerant; keep it moist, but not overly wet throughout the year.
**Fertilizing** Throughout the growing season.
**Transplanting/Soil** Every two to three years as required; use a smaller pot to keep the roots warm. It has fine roots so a small particle sized deciduous mix is ideal.
**Pests/Diseases** Generally pest free.
**Pruning/Styling** It can be pruned to shape. Wire the basic structure out and clip-and-grow the shoots to fill out, applying corrective wire as necessary. Thin out dense areas and heavy nodes with too many shoots.
**Propagation** From cuttings, or from seed.

## *Nothofagus*
## SOUTHERN BEECH

These are deciduous trees from the southern hemisphere that grow happily in temperate climates. They respond very well to clip-and-grow techniques. They are an underused species in the UK.
**Hardiness/Position** Frost hardy, zones 7–10. Protect in winter, but give full sun in summer.
**Watering** Do not allow it to dry out throughout the growing season. Keep it moist but not wet over winter. Do not allow it to sit in wet soil as it is susceptible to root rot.
**Fertilizing** Lightly throughout the year unless you want to push vigorous growth. If you are fertilizing heavily, ensure that a free-draining soil is used.
**Transplanting/Soil** Do this every two to three years in spring. Use a normal deciduous mix.
**Pests/Diseases** Fungal issues are a possibility; *Phytophthora* causes branch death.
**Pruning/Styling** As with other deciduous trees. Similar to Chinese elm, clip-and-grow

techniques work very well. Trim it to shape throughout the year.
**Propagation** Cuttings, seed.

### *Nothofagus antarctica* Antarctic beech
This has very small leaves, and delicate branching.

### *Nothofagus procera*
Fast-growing tree that offers rich autumn tints.

## *Olea*
# OLIVE
This is a very good species for bonsai: it is hardy, resilient, and responds well to bonsai techniques. It tolerates a wide climatic range, but thrives in very warm conditions. It can flower and fruit – but it is unusual to see this on bonsai – and will send out new shoots on old wood, even from the trunk. Dead wood features can be very hard and full of character. If you provide enough light and ventilation olives may be grown indoors, but it is better suited to outdoor cultivation.
**Hardiness/Position** Frost tender, zones 7–10. Protect from frosts, provide warmth, and olives grow all year round. Place them in full sun, even in the hottest conditions.
**Watering** It is drought tolerant but keeping it well watered allows the tree to thrive.
**Fertilizing** Do this throughout the growing season.
**Transplanting/Soil** Transplant every two years in warm climates, less frequently in colder ones. Use a free-draining soil; it grows well in a lava-based mix.
**Pests/Diseases** Generally pest free.
**Pruning/Styling** Olives respond well to pruning, but allow the shoots to extend before wiring and shaping, pruning back to shape. It can be defoliated if healthy. Secondary branching can be easily created through clip-and-grow techniques.
**Propagation** Cuttings of any size can be taken.

### *Olea europaea*
It has a slightly larger leaf size, which will reduce with cultivation.

### *Olea europaea* var. *sylvestris*
This very small-leaved variety is collected in parts of Spain, particularly Majorca. There are some incredible specimens with very dense branching and characterful dead wood.

## *Pemphis acidula*
# PEMPHIS
This shrub is found in tropical regions, especially in the Philippines. A coastal tree, it thrives if the foliage is sprayed with sea water daily. It is very vigorous, buds on old wood,

and sends out roots even if it is collected without any. It also responds well to regular pruning and defoliation.
**Hardiness/Position** Frost tender, zone 10, suitable for tropical and subtropical areas only. It will suffer under 13°C/55°F. Position it in direct sunlight all day.
**Watering** Do not allow it to dry out: it may be necessary to water three or four times a day.
**Fertilizing** Fertilize heavily and regularly for best results.
**Transplanting/Soil** A highly aerated soil is ideal, so use a lava rock-based mix. The roots are very tender so care must be taken with repotting. Washing the soil out of the pot and replacing works well.
**Pests/Diseases** Caterpillars and root nematodes can occur. Adding organic material such as crushed crab or lobster shells prevents this.
**Pruning/Styling** Wire the main skeleton shape and prune it to shape, using corrective wire to shape the main secondary branches.
**Propagation** Cuttings.

## *Picea*
# SPRUCE
Well suited to more northerly cool temperate climates, spruce can become characterful bonsai with small needles and dense foliage pads. The branches tend to develop in whorls and multiple shoots will grow from one node, so regular thinning out is important. Layer the branches and avoid styling them like junipers for good results. With correct care they send out adventitious buds, and shoot pinching in spring will push internal growth. Branches should be styled relatively straight, dropping down from the trunk.
**Hardiness/Position** Hardy, zones 2–7. It tolerates cold but protect pots from extensive freezing, and also from cold winds. It does best in dappled shade; keep it out of intense heat during the height of summer.
**Watering** Spruce does not like to be overly wet or dry, and has a moderate drought tolerance. Use a well-draining aerated soil mix, and water when the soil surface begins to dry.
**Fertilizing** Throughout the growing season.
**Transplanting** Once established, wait as long as you can – as long as the soil allows water to pass through; four to five years is ideal.
**Pests/Diseases** There can be fungal issues with needle cast if it is too humid or if there is poor air flow. Spruce spider mite is a problem in hot dry weather. Yellowing of the internal foliage is the first sign of these microscopic pests.
**Pruning/Styling** Allow the buds to break and begin to push out before pinching it back to leave a centimetre or two of the new growth.

New buds will then break further in the tree. Allow them to extend a little further before pinching again. Repeatedly doing this will build up foliage density on the branches. Thin out congested nodes to the two horizontally growing branches. Wire the branches in late autumn, but do not add too much exaggerated movement. Spread out and layer the secondary branches and then build up bulk through pinching and pruning. They are generally upright trees with straight trunks. Windswept and literati styles are appropriate.
**Propagation** From seed or cuttings.

### *Picea abies* Norway spruce
This is native to Europe, with slightly coarse foliage so it is suited for a larger tree. Many cultivars exist, including dwarf varieties.

### *Picea engelmannii* Engelmann spruce
Native to western North America, it has lovely blue green foliage and great bark characteristics on collected trees.

### *Picea glauca* White spruce, Alberta spruce
Found in northern North America and Canada, a number of ornamental dwarf cultivars exist which are used for bonsai.

### *Picea glehnii* Ezo spruce
Often confused with *P. jezoensis*, the two species are remarkably similar and come from the northernmost island of Japan and the Russian Sakhalin islands. Collected specimens exhibit compact foliage and great bark characteristics.

## *Pinus*
# PINE
This is one of the most common genera for bonsai, with a wide range of leaf, bark, and growth characteristics from varieties around the world. There are lots of variations in the care and cultivation for each type, and much is dependent on the location and vigour of the tree. One thing that is common is the importance of the root system. Pines rely on a strong healthy root system which has a large amount of beneficial mycorrhizae to assist the uptake of moisture and nutrients. Water and oxygen levels in the soil play an important part in this relationship. Energy balancing in the tree is very important to stop apical and terminal bud dominance. Pruning back strong growth to assist the weak is very important. Needle plucking can be done on some species to balance the amount of energy created in a branch by reducing the number of older needles. Never remove all the needles.

Pines prefer slightly acidic soil, so if your water is very base (hard water) then you may need to correct this with occasional ericaceous fertilizer. Pines are suitable for most coniferous styles and all sizes, but consider the natural growth habits and needle characteristics when choosing a style.

**Transplanting/Soil** Disturb as little as possible whilst maintaining a healthy root system in terms of air and moisture penetration. Try to maintain the rootball when transplanting, and remove the top surface and outer soil. A well-aerated, fast-draining conifer mix is ideal. Adding kiryu to the soil seems to promote high levels of mycorrhizae in the UK.

### Pinus contorta Lodgepole pine Very
cold tolerant species, they dislike year-round heat. Will back bud profusely given healthy conditions. Do not candle cut. Cultivate as for *P. sylvestris*.

### Pinus densiflora Japanese red pine
Similar to black pine (*P. thunbergii*), but treat feminine red pines more conservatively, particularly when styling. Red pines are more brittle, especially with age, so bend with great care. Use a well-aerated soil mix; it prefers to be slightly dry, but do not allow the soil to dry out completely. Apply a medium amount of fertilizer throughout the growing season unless candle cutting.

### Pinus mugo Mugo, mountain pine
This is the European pine, which is seen in garden centres. Cultivars often exhibit different growth habits and tend to be weaker or less suited to bonsai cultivation. Collected specimens are available across Europe and make very good trees. This is a flexible pine which buds profusely and given the correct care will create adventitious buds. Do not needle pluck too much; it tends to send out new buds at the base of needles. Thin out needles to create definition between bud clusters and a tidy appearance, but leave older needles where possible. Mugo has a tendency to create five or more buds at one spot, take care to thin out to two well-placed and evenly sized buds. Do not candle cut. Pinch as for *P. parviflora* in spring, and cut back strong shoots in autumn to promote adventitious budding. Increased ramification means reduced needle length.

**Hardiness/Position** Hardy, zones 3–10. Protect the tree from a hard, long freeze but it tolerates a wide range of climates. Give full sun and a well-ventilated position.

**Watering** Similar to black pine (*P. thunbergii*). Well aerated soil is essential.

**Fertilizing** Similar to white pine (*P. parviflora*).

**Transplanting/Soil** Better results seem to be had with autumn transplanting in late August or early September. Use standard pine mix.

**Pests/Diseases** Needle cast and woolly aphids are the biggest concern.

**Pruning/Styling** As white pine (*P. parviflora*).

**Propagation** Seed.

### Pinus parviflora Five needle pine, white pine This Japanese variety generally has smaller needles, creating a softer, more elegant and feminine feel. Needles are formed in bundles of five. They will elongate with excessive fertilizing and watering. Imported trees are often grafted on to black pine root stock to improve vigour and growth but do not be afraid of them on their own roots. They will struggle in extreme heat or a constantly wet environment. Moisture and oxygen levels in soil is key. They are reluctant to back bud unless very healthy, and will show signs of chlorosis or soil toxicity quite early. A number of dwarf *yatsubusa* cultivars and foliage types exist. Each has its idiosyncrasies.

**Hardiness/Position** Hardy, zones 4–7. Protect the tree from excessive moisture, especially over winter. It likes clean air, and will struggle in pollution. Full sun is best.

**Watering** Overwatering is the biggest issue, but do not allow the pot to dry out. Ensure a correct balance between moisture and oxygen throughout the year.

**Fertilizing** If your aim is compact growth and short needles, fertilize very little until the needles have fully extended and hardened off. Fertilize heavily after this, during late summer and autumn. Use a seaweed extract-style tonic to add micronutrients.

**Transplanting/Soil** As *Pinus*, above.

**Pests/Diseases** Woolly aphids (adelgids) are a big problem: look for white "fur" on the underside of branch tips. Spray with a systemic or contact killer. They will remain after they are dead, so clean and mark one or two branches to see if they return. Yellowing foliage is usually a sign of root or soil issues.

**Pruning/Styling** Do not candle cut. If growth is long in spring, pinch back or snap the tips of strong candles to leave some of the new very small needle-like growths on the stem. Balance the lengths of the candles by allowing weaker ones to elongate. Restricting terminal growth is equally important. Most varieties send out three shoots or buds – two weaker sideshoots/buds, and a stronger central one. If the sideshoots are viable, then in most circumstances remove the central shoot/bud. This should be done both in autumn, when the tree is setting buds, and also in spring or summer when the buds have opened and developed into shoots. Always look to assist the internal branches. They can be wired when the foliage is hard, but be careful of twisting the branches. Use any coniferous style, any size.

**Propagation** Seed; some varieties such as 'Zui-sho' will strike cuttings.

### Pinus ponderosa Native to western North
America, this has large, fleshy needles that will reduce in size with cultivation, and very flexible limbs. Superb craggy bark and hard dead wood can be seen on collected specimens. Hardy, zones 3–7, but protect it from a hard, long freeze. Keep in full sun and a well-ventilated position. Do not candle cut. Cultivate as for *P. mugo*.

### Pinus sylvestris Scots pine Found across
Europe and Asia, in many respects this pine is perfect for bonsai cultivation. Very vigorous, resilient, and tolerant, it sends out a profusion of buds, will ramify well, and the needle size will reduce with cultivation. It is an ideal species to start with and great results can be achieved. A number of cultivars exist; some dwarf cultivars such as 'Beuvronensis' make for very dense foliage pads. A single flush of growth is made each year, so candle cutting is not advised. It tolerates hard pruning and sends out adventitious buds when the terminal shoot is removed. It naturally forms a literati-type image. The biggest challenge is getting branches to set in position – wire quickly bites into the branches and may need to be removed after only a few months.

**Hardiness/Position** Hardy, zones 3–8. Protect it from a hard, long freeze but it is tolerant of a wide range of climates. Provide full sun and a well-ventilated position.

**Watering** Similar to black pine (*P. thunbergii*). Well-aerated soil is essential.

**Fertilizing** Similar to white pine (*P. parviflora*).

**Transplanting/Soil** Spring or autumn. Tolerant of a wide soil pH level but the best results come from a standard coniferous pine mix.

**Pests/Diseases** Needle cast and woolly aphids are the biggest concerns.

**Pruning/Styling** Similar to white and mugo pines. Young shoots can extend greatly; prune them back to shape and be conscientious about bud reduction and building up compact ramification by pruning vigorous growth off in favour of weaker internal buds. Wire secondary shoots into shape; once it has become well ramified shape with clip-and-grow techniques combined with occasional corrective wiring.

**Propagation** Seed.

### Pinus thunbergii Japanese black pine
Masculine black pines have long, thick, dark green needles and craggy bark.

**Hardiness/Position** Hardy, zones 5–10. Provide winter protection for the pots and delicate branches. It will tolerate frost but not prolonged freezing, and thrives in full sun.

**Watering** Use a well-aerated soil mix and do not allow the soil to dry out too much. Black pines thrive if they are given resources.

**Fertilizing** Fertilize heavily unless candle cutting.

**Transplanting/Soil** As *Pinus*, above.

**Pests/Diseases** Fungal problems like needle cast can occur if foliage is too moist overnight or air flow is poor. Spider mites, scale, and moth larvae are possible.

**Pruning/Styling** Black pines are very flexible and may be wired and bent to shape. Wire when new growth has hardened off in autumn or winter to minimize damage to shoots or needles. The new growth – candles – can have the tip pinched in spring or cut off entirely in summer (usually June), which causes a second flush of growth with smaller needles and shorter extensions. Only do this on healthy trees and in warm environments. This is a way to build up ramification, but always leave 8–10 pairs of needles on each branch. Look to prune back strong shoots where there is a weaker but viable sideshoot behind. This will cause adventitious budding, which in turn will increase ramification and compact the image.

**Propagation** Seed; layering is possible but will be slow to give results.

## *Podocarpus macrophyllus*
### CHINESE YEW, BUDDHIST PINE

A coniferous tree with *Taxus*-like foliage, although it is neither a pine nor a yew. It is often used as an indoor starter tree. Larger specimens are available in hot climates where it thrives. It will tolerate hard pruning.

**Hardiness/Position** Frost tender, zones 8–10. It thrives in warm climates; it can tolerate a light frost but provide protection once temperatures fall to 5°C (41°F). Full sun is best; place it near a window if you are growing it indoors.

**Watering** Keep it moist throughout the year but not too wet, especially if it is indoors. It is not overly drought tolerant.

**Fertilizing** Apply lightly throughout the growing season. For small leaves avoid fertilizing until growth has hardened off.

**Transplanting/Soil** Every three to four years, or as necessary. A moisture-retentive conifer mix is best for indoor trees; use something a little more free draining if it is outside. Roots are slow growing, so avoid heavy pruning.

**Pests/Diseases** Scale, sooty mould, mites, and root rot are possible problems.

**Pruning/Styling** Chinese yew is slow growing unless it is in a warm climate. Allow new growth to extend and then prune back to shape. This will cause adventitious buds and sideshoots to grow, which may then be pruned back. Defoliation of internal leaves without

touching the growing tips will result in forced budding; if this is done several times a year, then a very small leaf size can be achieved.

**Propagation** From cuttings or seed.

## *Potentilla fruticosa*
### POTENTILLA

This shrub is often used as a landscape plant but it has some ideal characteristics for bonsai: small leaves, flowers, and the ability to bud on old wood after a heavy prune. Branches may die from drought or frost but will generally grow back. However, if this happens too often, the tree eventually gives up. Lots of cultivars are available and material is available for collection from old gardens.

**Hardiness/Position** Hardy, zones 3–7. Protect it from frost in order to preserve branch structure and roots. Provide full sun unless it is in a small or shallow pot.

**Watering** Potentilla is not drought tolerant so ensure it is constantly moist throughout summer; do not overwater in winter.

**Fertilizing** Lightly throughout the year.

**Transplanting/Soil** Every two to three years in spring. Use water-retentive deciduous mix.

**Pests/Diseases** Generally pest free.

**Pruning/Styling** Potentilla can be pruned to shape. It will send out lots of buds and branches from the trunk: thin these out to build up structure, not silhouette. It will need almost weekly attention in hot weather to keep it compact. It has a live vein structure similar to junipers and when large branches die, you often see a hollow trunk, which adds interest. Branches may be wired and bent, but do so gently.

**Propagation** Seed, cuttings.

## *Prunus*
### ORNAMENTAL CHERRY

This is a wide-ranging genus of trees ideal for bonsai, and one that is particulary important to Japanese aesthetics. As it is a member of the rose family, there are potential problems with canker, as well as bacterial and fungal diseases. Some varieties are better suited for container cultivation than others. The best results are obtained by careful and patient cultivation and an appreciation of the naturally angular branching structure. Clip-and-grow techniques combined with correctional wiring will result in trees with superb natural character. Look for small-flowering varieties and do not allow them to fruit heavily, as this ruins branching structure and tires out trees.

**Hardiness/Position** Hardy, zones 3–10, depending on the species. Protect from heavy frosts and intense sunlight, but otherwise

prunus are strong trees. Full sun is best.

**Watering** They are thirsty trees, particularly during the growing season so never allow them to dry out.

**Fertilizing** Apply heavily in the growing season, except for older more mature trees where restricting growth is the objective.

**Transplanting/Soil** Every two to three years into a moisture- and nutrient-retentive soil mix. Spring is the ideal time to do this, after flowering and before bud break.

**Pests/Diseases** Fungal and bacterial problems are a concern so good hygiene is essential. Borers, scale, and caterpillars are also potentially troublesome.

**Pruning/Styling** Branches have a characteristic growth habit, so learn what it is before attempting to style. Young shoots are flexible but older branches become very brittle. Major bending is possible in the summer months. Adventitious budding is rare on many species, so prune back to two nodes in autumn to keep branching compact. They can be defoliated once leaves have hardened but this may affect flowering the following year. A patient clip-and-grow approach may be more rewarding. Do not over style prunus; embrace the wild nature and slightly chaotic branch growth.

**Propagation** Cuttings, seed, layering.

***Prunus avium* Wild cherry** As it ages, the smooth grey bark reddens, cracks, and peels adding great character, particularly to the winter image. It also offers plenty of value at other times of year with blossom, fruits, and spectacular autumn colours.

***Prunus cerasifera* Cherry plum** Blossoms from late winter into spring, producing masses of small white flowers on bare branches.

***Prunus incisa* Fuji cherry** This is a beautiful tree to work with, especially the variety 'Kojo-no-mai', which makes superb smaller sized trees.

***Prunus mahaleb* Mahaleb cherry, St Lucie cherry** Native to Mediterranean areas, this is a very vigorous tree which has a tendency to sprout on older wood.

***Prunus mume* Japanese flowering apricot** This is the queen of Japanese bonsai, and incredible bark quality can be seen on older trees, with superb natural branch movement and beautiful flowers in the middle of winter. There are hundreds of cultivars available: choose those with single, small flowers. 'Yabai', 'Hibai', and 'Koshuu Yabai' are most common in Japan.

**Prunus serrulata Flowering cherry**
Cherry blossom is an iconic Japanese image. Many cherry bonsai are made, but most are short lived as they are susceptible to fungal and bacterial problems. Look for weeping varieties and create a mass of branches to appreciate the beautiful spring flowers.

**Prunus spinosa Blackthorn, sloe** This is the best native prunus in the UK, and an ideal species for bonsai with superb character. Branches have small spikes, and the tree will set fruit if the flowers are left. Defoliation is possible but take care not to weaken the tree. Selective pruning is the best route to success.

**Prunus tomentosa Nanking cherry**
This is hardy and drought resistant but will thrive if well watered and protected in winter.

## Pseudocydonia sinensis
### CHINESE QUINCE
This deciduous tree belongs to the rose family. It has characteristic flaky bark, pink flowers in spring and may produce large yellow fruit if allowed. Branches take time to thicken, but will do so if the tree is vigorous. It prefers warmer climates but will tolerate frost.
**Hardiness/Position** Frost hardy, zones 5-8. Protect the tree from heavy frost and low temperatures. Full sun in summer is best.
**Watering** It is a very thirsty tree, so keep it well watered throughout summer, and moist but not wet in winter.
**Fertilizing** Apply fertilizer throughout the growing season after flowering; it will thrive on heavy fertilizer.
**Transplanting/Soil** Every two to three years or as necessary. Transplant after flowering. Use a moisture- and nutrient-retentive soil.
**Pests/Diseases** Fireblight and bacterial or fungal infections are the biggest concerns.
**Pruning/Styling** To maintain structure, allow new growth to extend to six or seven leaves before pruning back to two. Prune back branches in autumn after leaf drop. Young shoots are flexible but large branches are very brittle. Defoliation is not advised unless your plant is very vigorous, but leaf cutting to reduce the size by half reduces vigour at branch tips and allows light inside. Upright deciduous styles are best.
**Propagation** From seed or cuttings.

## Punica granatum
### POMEGRANATE
This is a slightly tender deciduous tree that is often seen with a twisted trunk in bonsai or collected tree from the Mediterranean. It flowers in summer followed by fruit in autumn. Care must be taken when removing large branches as dieback is a big problem.
**Hardiness/Position** Frost tender, zones 7-10. Protect it from frost and low temperatures. Full sun in summer is best.
**Watering** Keep pomegranate well watered especially when flowering or setting fruit. It should be moist but not wet in winter.
**Fertilizing** Apply throughout the growing season except during and after flowering. Once fruit has set, increase fertilizing.
**Transplanting/Soil** Later in spring once the temperature has risen and buds are beginning to swell and move. Carry out every two to three years, or as necessary. Avoid major root pruning if possible. Use a moisture- and nutrient-retentive soil.
**Pests/Diseases** Aphids and scale are potential problems.
**Pruning/Styling** If you are looking to maintain structure, allow new growth to extend to six or seven leaves before pruning back to two. To promote flowering, allow new growth to extend from summer until it sets flowers. Prune back branches in autumn after leaf drop. Young shoots are flexible but large branches are very brittle. Upright deciduous styles are best.
**Propagation** Seed, cuttings.

## Pyracantha
### FIRETHORN
This is an ideal species for bonsai in that they are very strong, have small leaves and fruit and are relatively easy to deal with. They are ideal for *shohin*-sized trees. Technically an evergreen, but it will drop old foliage before replacing it.
**Hardiness/Position** Frost tender, zones 7-10, although given winter protection it will grow elsewhere. Protect the tree once temperatures fall to 5°C (40°F). Full sun in summer is best. Birds may eat the fruit in winter.
**Watering** Keep it well watered throughout the growing season, and moist but not wet in winter.
**Fertilizing** Apply regularly throughout the growing season.
**Transplanting/Soil** Every two to three years for smaller trees, slightly longer for larger trees. A deciduous mix is suitable. Avoid disturbing the roots if possible.
**Pests/Diseases** Fireblight, aphids, and scale.
**Pruning/Styling** Pruning to shape with corrective wiring of the main branches. It grows vigorously and in all directions. Selective pruning and stopping new growth is essential. Suits any style; often seen as a cascade or group, and especially as *shohin*.
**Propagation** From cuttings or seed.

## Quercus
### OAK
This is a very distinctive and powerful deciduous genus, which has around 600 species. Many are suitable for bonsai, others less so. It can be difficult to reduce leaf size with some species. Style as you would deciduous trees. Dead wood features such as "stags horns" are possible. Some more vigorous varieties can be defoliated.
**Hardiness/Position** Frost hardy, zones 5-10 depending on the species. Protect from heavy freezing. Full sun and a well-ventilated position in summer is best.
**Watering** Keep moist throughout the year, but not wet.
**Fertilizing** For species where leaf size is an issue, wait until the leaves have fully hardened before fertilizing. For others, apply fertilizer lightly throughout the year unless rapid development is required. Branches can become coarse, so do not push too hard.
**Transplanting/Soil** Every two to three years for younger trees; more mature specimens will benefit from longer between transplanting, reducing leaf size and node length.
**Pests/Diseases** Powdery mildew is the biggest concern, so ventilation is a priority. It is not fatal but is visually unattractive.
**Pruning/Styling** Strong shoots will dominate if allowed to grow, so prune back vigorous shoots, either removing them entirely or cutting back to one leaf as soon as possible. Side and internal branches should be allowed to extend a little more before being stopped initially and then pruned back to one or two leaves once foliage has hardened off. Internal branches will suffer from lack of light so cut external leaves in half or defoliate to allow more light in. Wire branches loosely and shape. Directional pruning and bud selection are the best ways to develop ramification.
**Propagation** From seed or by layering.

**Quercus agrifolia Coast live oak**
The natural range is in California – the evergreen oak.

**Quercus cerris Turkey oak** This vigorous, fast-growing tree has downy leaves that provide autumn colour.

**Quercus faginea Portuguese oak** This deciduous or semi-evergreen is found in the western Mediterranean Balearic islands. It is hardy and tolerant of various soil conditions.

**Quercus ilex** Native to southern Europe, this evergreen oak will survive but not thrive in colder climates. It is a vigorous tree in warmth, and can be defoliated. It is apically dominant: be prepared to hold back growth.

**Quercus robur English oak** This slow growing tree is difficult but not impossible to ramify and reduce leaf size; it makes a very iconic British image.

**Quercus suber Cork oak** Similar to *Q. ilex*, but with very rugged cork bark.

## Rhododendron indicum
### SATSUKI AZALEA

A popular species for bonsai, these flowering shrubs are curiously addictive for enthusiasts despite them being somewhat horticulturally unforgiving. With a basic understanding of their needs and a slightly different approach, you can achieve success.

Azaleas are acid-loving shrubs that thrive in a specialist soil, Kanuma, which has an ideal pH level and water-retentive microstructure. Their roots are very fine and often become matted on the surface when a solid fertilizer is used. If water penetration becomes difficult, remove the crusty layer and replace with fresh soil. Try to not disturb the roots unless the soil becomes compacted. When transplanting, try to maintain a solid rootball and refrain from digging away at the core of the rootball underneath the trunk.

Basally dominant, the apex can weaken if water cannot penetrate directly underneath the trunk or if those roots are disturbed or pruned heavily. Prune the apex slightly more conservatively if there is a visible difference between the top and bottom.

It is important to maintain healthy, young secondary and tertiary branching; otherwise the overall vigour of the tree will suffer. Do not be afraid to prune the tree back hard if it is healthy. This maintains its good health, which will deteriorate if no pruning is done. Healthy trees can be hard pruned to no foliage – within a month new buds will appear all over the tree.

Satsuki azaleas flower in late spring or early summer and there is plenty of choice: hundreds of varieties are available in a multitude of different colours, shapes, and leaf sizes, and each has its own idiosyncrasy. Any style and size is possible but match leaf and flower size. Certain varieties will thicken very slowly, others very quickly. Other species, such as *R. obtusum* (Kurume azalea), are occasionally used, but the best results are gained from *R. indicum*, the satsuki azalea.
**Hardiness/Position** Hardy, zones 6–9. Protect it from heavy frosts. The bark is very thin and will crack, freeze, and seriously damage the tree. Provide full sun up to 32ºC (90ºF), then semi shade during midday heat.
**Watering** They are very thirsty shrubs, so never allow them to dry out dramatically.

Overwatering is possible; to avoid this be guided by the amount of foliage, the season, and the rate of the soil drying up.
**Fertilizing** Azaleas are hungry plants that will thrive on heavy fertilizing. Stop during flowering, otherwise fertilize throughout the growing season.
**Transplanting/Soil** Transplant as and when required based on the integrity of the soil surface. Avoid damaging the central root core but ensure water can penetrate underneath the trunk. Use small-sized Kanuma soil and plant in slightly larger than usual pots. Make sure the *nebari* is not close to the pot walls or too exposed on top. Spring is the best time for transplanting, although it is possible after flowering.
**Pests/Diseases** Spider mites, whiteflies, gall midge, scale, and leaf gall are the biggest worries. Look for uneven discolouration of leaves or leaf spots. Yellowing of foliage on the inside can also be chlorosis or malnutrition.
**Pruning/Styling** Azaleas can be manipulated into almost any style – even the most abstract shapes if desired – as its natural growth habit is to form clumps. Young branches up to 3 years old may be wired and bent but once they have become lignified they are very brittle. Hard pruning throughout the growing season will result in lots of buds, but the best time is after new growth starts in spring or after flowering when all flowers should be removed and branches pruned back hard. Ensure new foliage has the chance to harden off before any cold weather. See pp.122–125 for further details.
**Propagation** Cuttings are very successful.

### Rhododendron indicum 'Hakurei'
Has white flowers and small leaves.

### Rhododendron indicum 'Hoshi-no-kagayaki' Bears deep purple-coloured flowers and small leaves.

### Rhododendron indicum 'Kaho'
Offers large multicoloured flowers and larger oval leaves.

### Rhododendron indicum 'Kinsai'
Bears spidery red flowers, thin leaves, and tends to send out long shoots that need regular pruning.

### Rhododendron indicum 'Korin' Has pink star-shaped flowers and small leaves.

### Rhododendron indicum 'Osakazuki'
Has pink flowers, deep green leaves, and a very strong bushy form.

## Rosmarinus officinalis
### ROSEMARY

A fragrant species to work with, Rosemary can combine dramatic dead wood features with delicate foliage that, given the correct management, will create dense pads. It has a reputation for being difficult to work with, but with care and a delicate touch it will thrive. Native all across the Mediterranean, it will thrive in hot weather and requires only basic winter protection.
**Hardiness/Position** Frost tender, zones 7–10. Protected from hard frosts, they will be fine. Provide full sun in summer if it is growing actively.
**Watering** Rosemary is thirsty in summer heat, so do not allow it to dry out. It also remains active over winter even at low temperatures, so ensure that the soil is moist but not wet over winter.
**Fertilizing** Lightly throughout the growing season. Do not over fertilize.
**Transplanting/Soil** Delicacy is the key here; the roots are sensitive and will break away if treated too roughly. It has very fine feeder roots so a small particle size soil is ideal. A pumice-heavy coniferous mix works well. Once established, try to leave it in the pot for as long as possible.
**Pests/Diseases** Generally pest free.
**Pruning/Styling** Pruning is important: internal foliage will die off if it is allowed to constantly extend. Prune back only to what appears to be an active side bud. Do not prune back the whole tree all at once, especially in summer, because the actively growing tips are important for pulling moisture up from the roots. Treat similarly to a juniper in pruning back the growth and the results will be favourable. Wiring is possible, although older branches tend to be very brittle; try not to put too much movement into older branches.
**Propagation** Cuttings are usually very successful.

## Sageretia thea
### SAGERETIA

This is a common indoor species in Europe and North America. It has small oval leaves and rough bark. Tiny flowers are followed by blue berries.
**Hardiness/Position** Frost tender, zones 9–11. The ideal temperature is 12–18ºC (54–65ºF) during winter, 18–24ºC (65–75ºF) in summer. Sageretia needs a drop in temperature overnight. If you keep it indoors, take care not to overheat but make sure you provide plenty of sunlight.
**Watering** Do not allow it to dry out at any time of year, especially indoors. High humidity is ideal.

**Fertilizing** Apply throughout the growing season, less in winter.
**Transplanting/Soil** Every two to three years into a moisture-retentive indoor type mix.
**Pests/Diseases** Aphids, whiteflies and mildew are considerations.
**Pruning/Styling** Prune to shape constantly throughout the year. Prolific buds and branches are created so wiring can be avoided. Carry out directional pruning, then clip and grow.
**Propagation** Take cuttings.

## *Salix babylonica*
## WILLOW

This deciduous tree has a pleasing summer image. Look to recreate the delicacy of a weeping willow and avoid thick, heavy branching. Other species of willow are suitable; for the best results choose the small-leaved types.
**Hardiness/Position** Frost hardy, zones 5–9. Protect the tree from freezing.
**Watering** They are very thirsty trees, and will not object to standing in water throughout summer. Do not make the tray too shallow or it will overheat and boil the roots. Keep moist but not wet in winter.
**Fertilizing** Apply regularly throughout the growing season.
**Transplanting/Soil** Transplant annually or even twice a year if very vigorous. Use a basic deciduous soil mix.
**Pests/Diseases** Aphids, caterpillars, and scale are potential problems.
**Pruning/Styling** Allow shoots to extend, then manipulate them downwards by hand, or wire them into a weeping style. The branches thicken quickly so take care not to cause wire damage. Prune hard in autumn back to an upward pointing bud. Tertiary branches are replaced every year.
**Propagation** Cuttings are easy to strike – the thicker the better.

## *Serissa japonica*
## TREE OF A THOUSAND STARS

This is an indoor tree for northern climates. The bark and roots have an unpleasant smell and it can be difficult to cultivate. Positioning is key. It has very small flowers and dense branching.
**Hardiness/Position** Frost tender, zones 8–11. If grown indoors, find a location that is not too cold, has no draughts and is humid. Close to a radiator is not good as it will dry the tree out.
**Watering** Do not allow it to dry out; keep it moist year round, but not constantly wet. Allow the surface of soil to dry a little before watering. Misting the foliage helps.

**Fertilizing** Apply lightly throughout the growing season.
**Transplanting/Soil** Every two to three years into a basic indoor mix.
**Pests/Diseases** Scale. Yellowing foliage is often due to poor positioning.
**Pruning/Styling** Prune to shape constantly throughout the year. Prolific buds and branches are created so wiring is not necessary. Use directional pruning, and a clip-and-grow approach.
**Propagation** Cuttings.

## *Stewartia monadelpha*
## STEWARTIA

This elegant deciduous tree with flaky copper bark has autumnal colour and flowers in summer. It can be a bit difficult to keep in colder climates.
**Hardiness/Position** Frost hardy, zones 6–9. Protect from heavy freezing, and ideally from all frost. Best in full sun except in midsummer when it appreciates midday shade.
**Watering** Do not allow it to dry out throughout growing season, and keep moist but not wet in winter.
**Fertilizing** As for maples (*Acer*); wait until growth has hardened off.
**Transplanting/Soil** Every two to three years, in spring; use a deciduous mix.
**Pests/Diseases** Generally pest free.
**Pruning/Styling** Carry out deciduous styling; this is ideal for upright forms, and gives elegant trees with upward growing branches and delicate ramification.
**Propagation** Seed, cuttings.

## *Tamarix chinensis*
## TAMARISK

This deciduous shrub/small tree has characteristic wispy feather-like foliage that is pendulous. Style in similar way to willow; branches will die off at the end of the year. A weeping style ideal but there are some incredible collected specimens out there with dead wood features.
**Hardiness/Position** Frost hardy, zones 7–10. Protect from harsh frost, and provide full sun in summer unless watering is an issue.
**Watering** Keep moist constantly throughout summer; it is a very thirsty tree. Keep moist but not waterlogged over winter.
**Fertilizing** Throughout the growing season.
**Transplanting/Soil** Annually if necessary; otherwise every two to three years in a coniferous type well-aerated mix. Transplant in spring as the buds swell.
**Pests/Diseases** Generally pest free.
**Pruning/Styling** As for willow (*Salix*).
**Propagation** Cuttings, layering.

## *Taxodium distichum*
## BALD CYPRESS

This has a very characteristic flat top growth habit and a huge flaring root buttress. It is a deciduous conifer with wispy foliage that grows naturally in swamps.
**Hardiness/Position** Hardy, zones 4–10. Protect it from extreme cold. Provide partial shade in extreme heat in summer, and full sun in more temperate climates.
**Watering** Keep wet all year; they tolerate anaerobic swamps, but do not need to be sitting in water constantly.
**Fertilizing** Heavily during the growing season.
**Transplanting/Soil** Transplant during the dormant period. Use a suitable coniferous mix that will hold moisture well but also aerate the soil.
**Pests/Diseases** Generally pest free.
**Pruning/Styling** Young branches tend to grow upwards but the desired effect is for downward sweeping branches. They can be torn from the upper side of the branch socket if necessary. Cover heavy branches that need bending with raffia to protect them before applying wire. Prune back growth in summer to promote adventitious budding.
**Propagation** Cuttings are most successful.

## *Taxus*
## YEW

A commonly used conifer for bonsai, which is ideally suited for slightly overcast and wet climates – they thrive in the UK. A healthy tree will bud profusely even from the trunk. Foliage pads are relatively easy to build up once a basic skeleton structure is in place through regular pinching of new growth and pruning to stimulate adventitious budding. Removal of some older foliage can result in adventitious budding, but do not reduce the foliage mass too much. Soft dead wood features such as hollow trunks may be seen on cultivated trees, although *yamadori* collected trees may show very hard wood. Like juniper, yew exhibits a linear root-live vein-branch relationship.
**Hardiness/Position** Hardy, zones 4–8. Protect from deep freezing as roots are fleshy and tender. Full sun is fine during spring and autumn, but protect it from intense summer heat under partial shade.
**Watering** Keep on the moist side throughout the year; like junipers they can tolerate dry conditions but will thrive with regular watering. A well-aerated soil mix will prevent too much moisture being retained – they dislike constantly wet roots and will succumb to root rot.
**Fertilizing** Apply regularly throughout the growing season.

**Transplanting/Soil** Similar to juniper. The roots tend to be quite delicate and tender, especially on collected trees. Be conservative with root pruning and soil removal.
**Pests/Diseases** Scale and root rot are the only major concerns. Scale is difficult to detect as they look like buds forming on the stems.
**Pruning/Styling** Generally slightly less dramatic than juniper, but dead wood features are always interesting. They can be wired and bent fairly easily, although thicker branches are difficult to manipulate. Creating a layered skeleton branching structure and then allowing shoots to grow before pinching to promote budding is best. Do not over wire young branches; directional pruning and conscientious pinching will soon create well ramified pads. Eventually the branches will be very compact and upward growing.
**Propagation** From cuttings or layering.

**Taxus baccata European yew** Dark green foliage and red berries are possible in autumn. It is ideally suited to the northern European climate. There are over 200 ornamental cultivars, but many are too weak or unsuitable for bonsai cultivation.

**Taxus cuspidata Japanese yew**
Displaying a slightly lighter shade of green, it is a little less vigorous than the *T. baccata*. Many imported specimen trees exist.

## *Tsuga*
## HEMLOCK
This conifer is similar in many ways to *Taxus*, preferring colder, wetter, shadier climates. Treat and create in very similar way.
**Hardiness/Position** Hardy, zones 3–7. Protect from cold winds in winter and from deep freezes. Give partial shade in hot climates.
**Watering** Similar to *Taxus*, it prefers moist soil, that is not waterlogged.
**Fertilizing** Regularly throughout the season
**Transplanting/Soil** Try to leave undisturbed if the soil is relatively porous, and transplant as necessary. Use a coniferous mix.
**Pests/Diseases** Generally pest free.
**Pruning/Styling** Pinch the tips of new growth throughout the season to maintain the shape. Allow new shoots to extend, wire to shape and then pinch the tips to create adventitious buds. Let them extend before repeating. Wire will easily dig in: take care to avoid this. The growth habit is often multi-trunked or a slender trunk with spreading branches. Dramatic collected specimens do exist.
**Propagation** From seed or from cuttings.

**Tsuga canadensis Eastern hemlock**
Often multi-trunked with graceful foliage.

**Tsuga heterophylla Western hemlock**
Bears short, glossy, needle-like leaves that darken with age.

## *Ulmus*
## ELM
This deciduous tree makes an ideal bonsai due to its rapid ramification. It can be a very vigorous grower, so quick results can be obtained especially with patience and dedication to very fine work. It tolerates repeated defoliation, which creates very small leaves.
**Hardiness/Position** Frost hardy, zones 5–9. Protect pots from frost. Provide full sun up to 32°C (90°F), except in the most intense conditions.
**Watering** Keep moist throughout the year for best results. Do not overwater if it is grown indoors.
**Fertilizing** Regularly throughout the growing season. It will not affect the node length and leaf size too much, but do not over fertilize if you are looking for compact ramification.
**Transplanting/Soil** Every two to three years. Balance the root growth early on in development: imported trees often have one or two strong roots, which should be pruned back in favour of weaker side roots. Use a deciduous mix.
**Pests/Diseases** Aphids and gall mites are a slight concern.
**Pruning/Styling** A clip-and-grow approach is key. Allow new shoots to extend out if thickness is desired before pruning back to one or two nodes. When building up ramification, allow shoots to extend to three or four leaves before pruning back to two leaves. Once they harden off, defoliate. New shoots will come out again, so repeat the process. This can be done numerous times throughout the year, but give thought to less defoliation on weaker internal branches to build up their strength. Wire branches to set the initial structure, then build using directional pruning. Hard cuts can be made in autumn. It can be made into any style or size.
**Propagation** From cuttings or by layering.

**Ulmus glabra Wych Elm** A rounded tree with grey-brown bark and yellow autumn foliage.

**Ulmus x hollandica 'Jacqueline Hillier'**
This dwarf variety has a very dense natural habit and tiny leaves, so is ideal for small size bonsai.

**Ulmus parvifolia Chinese elm** One of the most common starter trees available, this can be grown indoors on a well-lit windowsill as well as outdoors: it is very hardy. Although deciduous, as an indoor tree it often holds onto its leaves all year round. With careful work, Chinese elms can be trained into remarkable specimen trees over a number of years. They are an underrated species due to their often very humble beginnings.

**Ulmus procera English elm** An upright tree with grey brown bark and dark green leaves that turn yellow in autumn.

## *Wisteria*
## WISTERIA
This deciduous climber will flower in summer with large racemes of usually purple flowers.
**Hardiness/Position** Frost hardy, zones 4–9. Protect pots from frost. Provide full sun except in the most intense conditions up to 32°C (90°F).
**Watering** Wisteria are very thirsty trees in summer: allow them to stand in a deep tray of water during midsummer. Keep moist but not wet in winter.
**Fertilizing** Apply heavily to promote vegetative growth, but give zero nitrogen fertilizer to promote flowering.
**Transplanting/Soil** Leave wisteria to become pot bound and force maturity if you want it to flower; allowing roots to grow will promote foliage and branch development. Use water and nutrient-retentive soil. Transplant in spring.
**Pests/Diseases** Aphids and scale are possible problems.
**Pruning/Styling** It is difficult to build ramification in the traditional sense of the word; prune growth after flowering and then as and when new shoots extend. Hard prune in autumn if it is dramatically out of shape. Style in a way that shows off the flowers rather than creating a structure.
**Propagation** From cuttings or layering.

## *Zelkova serrata*
## JAPANESE ELM
This is very similar to other elms in approach and care. It is almost always styled as broom style, but does not have to be exclusively so. See *Ulmus*, above.

# Glossary

Several of the Japanese words that are in general use in the bonsai world exist in most languages simply because they are much more succinct or easily understood than their translations. Some are definitely worth keeping; others are easily replaced.

## Size terms

These are rough categories and it is more about a feeling rather than getting the tape measure out.

**Mame** The smallest size, up to and around 10cm (4in).
**Shohin** Small trees up to and around 25cm (10in).
**Kifu** Medium trees, up to 35cm (14in).
**Chuhin** Medium trees up to 45cm (18in).

Larger trees are technically called *oogata* or *oomono* but in practice these terms are very rarely used: the lack of a prefix implies the tree is larger than *chuhin*.

## Other Japanese terms

**Jin** A dead wood feature created from a branch. A *tenjin* is one which extends above and beyond the foliage canopy.
**Shari** A dead wood feature on the trunk, the exposed bone of the tree.
**Uro** A hollow feature, often as part of dead wood in the trunk, often seen in *Taxus*.
**Nebari** The surface roots and the lower trunk area. Sets the feeling and direction of the tree.
**Yamadori** A tree collected from the wild, literally "Taken from mountain".
**Mochikomi** The subtle sense of age, character and refinement that a tree takes on after many years of cultivation as a bonsai in a container.

## Horticultural and other terms

**Accent plant** (also: Companion plant, *Kusamono*, *Shitakusa*) A smaller plant displayed with a bonsai which accentuates the season or helps in creating a cohesive and interesting image.

**Adventitious bud** (also: Back bud) A bud which develops on a branch or trunk, anywhere except the apical meristem, or growing tip of the branch. These buds are essential for bonsai development.

**Apex** The top of the tree, formed generally from a number of branches. Trees tend to grow upwards and show apical dominance, a character determined by auxin production.

**Auxin** Hormones in plants which control growth. Auxins produced in the apex/terminal growth restrict the growth of buds closer inside the tree. Pruning branch tips will remove the auxin-producing buds and promote back budding.

**Branching** "Primary" branches are those growing directly from the trunk, and "secondary" branches or shoots are those which then split off from those primary branches. "Tertiary" branches are the fine branch tips also referred to as ramification.

**Callus** The cells that form over a wound. Analogous to a scab, the ideal situation is for it to heal over very quickly and attractively so that ultimately it is not noticed.

**Candle** The new shoots on pine trees, at the stage of elongation before the needles open up and develop. Candles may be cut off entirely or have the tip pinched off to regulate growth, depending on species.

**Defoliation** The intentional removal of leaves on a deciduous tree to stimulate further growth, increase ramification, and decrease leaf size.

**Desiccation** Drying out through lack of water. May refer to leaves, roots or the live vein.

**Dieback** Fatal branch or trunk damage caused by disease, damage, or most likely hard pruning.

**Foliage** The green leaves or needles on the tree. The foliage type is an important consideration for bonsai: small, compact foliage is very desirable.

**Grafting** Propagation technique that joins plant tissue together. In bonsai this is more often done to improve branch placement: buds and branches can be grafted into ideal positions, and foliage may be developed on leggy branches. Approach, bud, and thread grafting techniques are used.

**Internode** Distance between two nodes. On deciduous trees internodal distances should reduce as you move out along the branch to the tips.

**Juvenile foliage** Usually seen only on juniper species. Young shoots have a spiky, needle-like structure; the more desirable softer, fleshier mature foliage is known as scale foliage. Juvenile foliage grows when the tree is in quick need of energy generated by photosynthesis. Excessive pruning or root stress often triggers a massive burst of juvenile growth.

**Leader** The strong apical shoot, either at the top of the trunk or at the tip of a branch.

**Lime sulphur** Used in a dilution of 1 part lime sulphur to 2 or 3 parts water in order to "bleach" white dead wood and also to help preserve it by killing bacteria or fungi in the wood.

**Mycelium, mycorrhizae** A symbiotic beneficial relationship between a fungus and the roots of a plant, most commonly seen on pines but present in almost all species. The fungi need an aerobic environment to thrive so the balance between oxygen and water inside the pot is important.

**Negative space** The space around and in between the subject or subjects in the image. This an important element in the composition of bonsai: empty space not only adds depth to the display, but also introduces a sense of mystery, movement, or simplicity.

**Node** The point on a plant stem from which buds, leaves, and branches form. A fundamental concept in bonsai is to avoid having too many branches coming from one node; on deciduous trees the ideal maximum is two.

**Pinching** A form of pruning in which tender growth is removed by hand, pinched off by the fingers and thumb. It should not be performed across an entire tree the way a goat grazes. For best results with many species, especially junipers, pinching is not advised.

**Pot-bound** A situation where the roots have filled the pot, the soil surface has become very hard, and there is no room for new roots to grow. For a mature bonsai, the stage just before this is ideal for restricting growth and reducing leaf size – however a tree should never become so pot-bound that it weakens beyond recovery.

**Ramification** A structure formed of branches. Generally refers to the finer twigs that form the tertiary branching at the ends of deciduous trees. The ideal structure is for branches to split into two, then again in two, then into two again... and so on, including changes of thickness and direction.

**Soil** Generic term for the growing medium used in bonsai. This is not the same as soil from your garden but usually a specialized mix of inorganic substrates which serve different purposes (*see p.41*).

**Systemic** In reference to pesticide or fungicide, a chemical that is absorbed by the plant, either through the roots or foliage and kills pests from the inside out when attacked. The other type is a contact killer, which works when it makes direct contact with pests.

**Taper** To reduce in thickness towards one end. Trunks or branches without taper can appear very young and uninteresting. Taper is generally achieved by cutting back to a thinner branch and allowing that to grow out and become the new leader.

# Index

# Resources

## Clubs and societies
Good places to find out about local clubs and bonsai shows.

Bonsai Clubs International (BCI)
www.bonsai-bci.com

### UK and Europe
European Bonsai Association (EBA)
www.ebabonsai.com

Federation of British Bonsai Societies (FOBBS)
www.fobbsbonsai.co.uk

Noelanders Trophy (Belgium)
www.bonsaiassociation.be/en/trophy.php

Unione Bonsaisti Italiani (Italy)
www.ubibonsai.it

### US and Canada
American Bonsai Society (ABS)
www.absbonsai.org

Bonsai Societies of Florida (BSF)
bonsai-bsf.com

Golden State Bonsai Federation
www.gsbf-bonsai.org

Mid Atlantic Bonsai
midatlanticbonsai.freeservers.com

World Bonsai Friendship Federation (WBFF)
www.northamericanbonsaifederation.com

## Magazines and blogs
Bonsai eejit blog
bonsaieejit.com/blog/

Bonsai Focus
www.bonsaifocus.com

International Bonsai
www.internationalbonsai.com

Bonsai Art (German)
www.bonsai-art.com

Esprit Bonsai (French)
www.esprit-bonsai.com

## UK nurseries
Peter Warren, Saruyama Bonsai London  www.saruyama.co.uk

Peter Snart, Willowbog Bonsai Hexham, Northumberland
www.willowbog-bonsai.co.uk

Peter Chan, Herons Bonsai Lingfield, Surrey
www.herons.co.uk

Ken Leaver, Windybank Bonsai Carshalton, Surrey
www.windybankbonsai.co.uk

Ian Cuppleditch, British Bonsai Storrington, West Sussex
www.britishbonsai.co.uk

Steve Tolley Bonsai Kidderminster, Worcestershire
www.stevetolleybonsai.com

Corin and Paul Tomlinson, Greenwood Bonsai Studio, Nottingham  www.bonsai.co.uk

Graham Potter, Kaizen Bonsai Great Yarmouth, Norfolk
www.kaizenbonsai.com

Lee Verhorevoort Bonsai Bexleyheath, Kent
www.lvbonsai.co.uk

## European artists
David Benavente, Spain
www.davidbenavente.com

Valentin Brose, Germany
www.brosebonsai.com

Marco Invernizzi, Italy
www.marcoinvernizzi.com

Marc Noelanders, Belgium

Kevin Willson, UK
www.kevinwillsonbonsai.com

## US nurseries
Ryan Neil, International Bonsai Mirai, Portland, Oregon
www.bonsaimirai.com

Michael Hagedorn, Crataegus Bonsai, Portland, Oregon
crataegus.com

Zack and Bob Shimon, Mendocino Coast Bonsai, California
mcbonsai.com/wp

International Bonsai Arboretum William N. Valavanis, Rochester, New York
www.internationalbonsai.com

Jim Doyle, Nature's Way Nursery Harrisburg, Pennsylvania
www.natureswaybonsai.com

Brussel Martin, Brussel's Bonsai Olive Branch, Mississippi
www.brusselsbonsai.com

Michael Feduccia, Feduccia's Bonsai, Plant City, Florida
feducciasbonsai.com

## Pots
John Pitt Bonsai Ceramics:
www.johnpittbonsaiceramics.co.uk

Walsall Studio Ceramics:
www.walsall-studio-ceramics.com

Stone Monkey Ceramics:
stonemonkey1968.wordpress.com

Ron Lang: www.langbonsai.com

Sara Rayner: www.redwing.net/~daalms